Chris O'Connell

STREET TRILOGY

CAR
RAW
KID

Street Trilogy was first performed on 8th February 2005 at Warwick Arts Centre, Coventry, in a co-production between Theatre Absolute and Warwick Arts Centre.

Street Trilogy

Complete cast

Car

Jason	**Lee Colley**
Nick	**Peter Ash**
Tim	**Daniel Harcourt**
Mark	**Sean Cernow**
Gary	**Graeme Hawley**
Robert	**James Low**

Raw

Lex	**Rachel Brogan**
Trainers	**Samantha Power**
Addy	**Peter Ash**
Lorna	**Rebekah Manning**
Rueben	**Graeme Hawley**
Shelley	**Belinda Everett**

Kid

Lee	**Lee Colley**
Zoe	**Samantha Power**
K	**Sean Cernow**
Bradley	**Rebekah Manning**

Production team

Writer	**Chris O'Connell**
Director	**Mark Babych**
Producer	**Julia Negus**
Youth Arts Director	**Georgina Egan**
Trainee Director	**Paul Simpson**
Set and Costume design	**Janet Vaughan**
Lighting design	**James Farncombe**
Original soundscapes	**Andy Garbi**
Stage Manager	**Stephen Cotton**
Technician and relights	**Will Evans**
Marketing and PR	**Chamberl**...
	admin@ ... ·.com
	020 7 ...

theatre
absolute

Theatre Absolute is a multi-award winning new writing theatre company. Founded in 1992, by Chris O'Connell and Julia Negus, and based in Coventry, the company commissions, produces and tours new plays which are bold, uncompromising and contemporary. Theatre Absolute's work delivers a hard edged aesthetic that is founded on a strong and heightened narrative.

Individually, the three plays in *Street Trilogy* have performed to great acclaim across the UK and Europe, won two Scotsman Fringe Firsts at the Edinburgh Festival for Outstanding New Work, and a Time Out Live Award for Best New Play on the Fringe, establishing Theatre Absolute as leaders at the hard edge of new writing.

Theatre Absolute would like to thank:
Alan Rivett and Neil Darlison at Warwick Arts Centre for their faith in the company's work, Alison Gagen for her encouragement at ACE West Midlands, David Edgar and the trustees from Sir Barry Jackson Trust, Clare Huby at Coventry City Council, Ian and Graham at Coventry Rugby Football Club, Clair, Jill and Ben from Chamberlain AMPR, Katie Haines, Theatre Absolute's associate artists and board members, Reuben and Joe, Sheila and Terry, Helen and Pete and Andrew Moore. Thanks also to: Jane Hytch and Clare Maddocks at the Belgrade Theatre, to Debbie Kingsley, to Mark Babych, the director of the trilogy whose work has shone and grown when things have felt unstagable and unworkable, to the influence of Jeremy Weller, to John Ginman, for dramaturgy, to all the designers and technicians who have worked on the trilogy, to Ian Tilton for photos when there wasn't always enough cash, to Paul and Koo at Through and Through for their brilliant poster designs, and to all the actors involved with the trilogy, both past and present, who have revelled in the work, and gone on to claim the plays for themselves with a dedication to the cause that has been fantastic to witness.

Foreword

Brutality, fear, self loathing, and a need for belonging underpin the deep cry of pain, and search for love that characterise the mesmeric world and haunted souls of Chris O'Connell's *Street Trilogy*.

From the adrenaline fuelled anarchy and chaos of *Car*, the unrelenting physical and psychologically damaged world of *Raw*, to the potential of a new beginning in *Kid*, all three plays seek to capture the texture and rhythm of lives caught in the claustrophobia of unremitting violence, exploring the difficulties of change as the characters attempt to relinquish themselves from the crushing pain of their existence.

These are not merely plays that seek to paint vulnerable young people as victims of a world that doesn't care. Nor does it simply bracket the adult world as misguided saviours hell bent on wrapping these damaged individuals in a woolly blanket of liberal understanding. Whilst there is no doubt of the emotional punch that the plays pack to an audience, often stretching and tugging at our sense of injustice and sympathy for those less fortunate, the world of the street trilogy is tough, disturbing and morally complex, often swinging between sympathy and loathing for both victim and offender, until the moral ground between them becomes blurred and ambiguous. In *Car*, a fire rages out of control, and as the two parties seek a resolution to their conflict, and ultimately fail, the fire threatens to engulf the city and its inhabitants, suggesting that if no dialogue can be found then we all burn, regardless of our respective backgrounds.

Making this trilogy has involved seven years of collaborative work between myself, Theatre Absolute, and the many artists that have helped Chris O'Connell and Julia Negus shape their vision for a company dedicated to creating dynamic and visceral work. I am struck by the epic nature of the storytelling. These are huge geographic and psychological landscapes that transport the audience into a myriad of physical and mental locales, both real and imagined. I am reminded of the poetics and verbal pyrotechnics contained within the vocabulary of Lex, Jason and K. Monologues, poetic and tortuous, that shine a light into the inner sanctums of their brutalised violent psyches, revealing a latent and extraordinary genius of imagination, that if only channelled and redirected away from violence, could produce extraordinary human beings.

Mark Babych
Director – *Street Trilogy*
January 2005

Introduction

In 1990, I went to work with Jeremy Weller, in Edinburgh. A director and a deviser, he was one of the founder members of The Grassmarket Project, a company with a style and a vision dedicated to a kind of theatre verité. I was one of the few professional actors he was working with; he offered me £100 a week and free accommodation to work on a play called *Glad*. It was made in three months, with, about and featuring the homeless of Edinburgh's Grassmarket – a strip of road in the city centre which at the time was a grim mile of homeless hostels and buzz eyed people who you would walk past in dread of them telling you their story. But Jeremy's work is all about stories, and other plays I did with him – *Bad*, 1991, in a Young Offenders Institute in Falkirk; *The Plague*, Berlin, 1992, with some of the city's homeless; and *The Foolish Young Man*, Munich, 1994, with street gangs – were all about stories and a wild realisation, for me, of the function of theatre. They were stories of those dispossessed of a voice, who were surviving the pressure of a life outside the 'inside'. This world of pressure was incredible, extreme, brittle, highly charged, and compelling.

My attachment to the work I did in Edinburgh led me to work in the mid-1990s in the probation service, in Coventry. I entered the work as an idealist, believing that with committed emotional investment people breaking the law can be helped to change. The offenders I met were often grudging, threatening, vulnerable, funny, sad, and very rarely grateful. Why should they be? My idealism hit a brick wall. I wanted to grab people by the throat and tell them they were wasting their lives. It is this work and these frustrations which inspired *Street Trilogy*, which I began writing with *Car*, in 1999.

A whirlwind of crime has ripped through the modern world, and no one can agree when, or why it happened. Good citizens are afraid, they're afraid in their homes, and the country is at war with itself. But it's not enough to threaten short sharp shocks and build more prisons while doing nothing serious to tackle the blight at the heart of countless lives in what is an unequal society. And how *do* people on the wrong side of the law, actually change? Is it purely about personal choice, 'getting on your bike', getting a job, or are people trapped by their environment? No matter what arguments there are against it, it's hard to ignore the unforgiving notion of cause and effect.

Beyond the above ideas, theatricality has been a prerequisite in the making of the trilogy. Whenever the plays have been performed in youth centres or in a theatre where there's a large percentage of 'kids', the feedback has sometimes led to cries of there not being enough of a police presence, that the police are everyday life, 'banging on the door'. Accepted, but I never wanted to go down that route: the staid naturalism of TV's *The Bill* with a bolshie cop and a Sarf London thug. My experience in Edinburgh and in probation left me with the impression that no one is just a car thief, no one is just a mugger, and no one is just a victim. The internal landscape of crime and punishment is huge, complex, and in these plays often poetic, as the characters give expression to the interior worlds we *all* live in.

Each of the plays thrives on the stylised, on 'what ifs'. It isn't interesting to say "so and so wouldn't do that", but to ask instead "WHAT IF so and so did this, or did that, what would happen then?" In moments of extremity, people will do anything. The point at which each play begins is highly intense; the characters don't appear, and then get unhappy, the pressure is there from the word go.

Car, *Raw* and *Kid* have a personal and thematic journey. From start to end, my progress as a writer is visible on the page, and the theme pursued through each of the plays, change, and the possibility of change, becomes most resonant in the final play as Lee and Zoe stand on the verge of one of the ultimate changes in anyone's life: the birth of a new child, and the prospect of parenting.

I hope *Street Trilogy* is a compelling read, and say a huge thanks to Theatre Absolute and producer Julia Negus for such dedication and unswerving determination to raise the appropriate amounts of cash, but also for her vision in sticking by the three plays which have taken seven years to complete.

Chris O'Connell
January 2005

Actors and Production Team

Chris O'Connell – Writer

After winning a Pearson Television Theatre Writers Bursary, Chris was Writer-in-Residence for Paines Plough, 1999–2000. Plays for Theatre Absolute include: *Car*, *Raw* and *Kid*, *Big Burger Chronicles*, and *She's Electric*. Other recent work by Chris includes: *Tall Phoenix*, for Belgrade Theatre; *Thyestes*, for RSC; *Hymns*, for Frantic Assembly; *Hold Ya'*, for Red Ladder Theatre Co; *Auto*, for Vanemuine Theatre, Estonia; *Southwark*, for Paines Plough; *Cool Water Murder*, for Belgrade Theatre; *The Blue Zone*, for mac Productions; and *Gabriel's Ashes* for BBC Radio 4. His work has been both read and produced in Estonia, Italy, Australia and America. Chris is currently Playwright in Residence at Birmingham University, attached to their M(Phil) in playwrighting.

Julia Negus – Producer

Trained at Webber Douglas Academy of Dramatic Art, London, Julia co-founded Theatre Absolute in 1992 with writer Chris O'Connell. Julia has produced all of the company's work to date.

Mark Babych – Director

Mark's extensive theatre credits have seen him direct a wide variety of work from classics to new writing, both in the UK and abroad. He has been involved in the creation and direction of the entire *Street Trilogy* since its inception in 1999, and is thrilled to have the opportunity to finally put all three works together.

Mark is also Artistic Director of the Octagon Theatre, Bolton, which since his appointment in 1999 has won several awards for the range and quality of its work. His numerous productions at the Octagon include: *Frankie and Johnny in the Clare de Lune*, *Twelfth Night*, *Kindertransport*, *Four Nights In Knaresborough*, *Little Malcolm And His Struggle Against The Eunuchs*, *The Weir*, *Cooking With Elvis*, *The Lonesome West* and *Neville's Island*; and at Worcester Swan Theatre where he was Associate Director, his productions include *They're Playing Our Song*, *Who's Afraid Of Virginia Woolf?*, *Talking Heads*, *Macbeth* and *Hard Times*.

As a freelance director, Mark's productions include *HAM!* (New Vic, Newcastle-under-Lyme); *AUTO* (Vanemuine Theatre, Tartu, Estonia); *Happy Jack*, *Distinguished Service*, *Kissing Sid James*, *RSVP*, *Graceland* and *Heart And Soul* all for the Coliseum Theatre, Oldham; and *Phil And Jill And Jill And Phil*, *Silas Marner* and *Wakey! Wakey! In Bed With Billy Cotton*, Belgrade Theatre, Coventry.

Georgina Egan – Youth Arts Director

Having worked professionally as an actor with small touring companies for five years, Georgina moved to Ireland and studied Youth and Community work at St Patrick's University in Maynooth. During her stay in Ireland she worked in community arts, as a drama worker with young offenders and in outreach work with the Travelling community. In 1998, she set up the Coventry City Mentoring Project with Community Education. She spent five years managing The Acting Out Project, a partnership with the Belgrade Theatre and the LEA that is now used nationally as a model of best practice for work related learning provision – offering a 'BTEC First Diploma in Performing Arts' course for year 10 & 11 students. Georgina is a freelance theatre practitioner, currently working with the Birmingham Rep Theatre, and is Theatre Absolute's Youth Arts Director.

Janet Vaughan – Set and Costume Design

Janet Vaughan trained in Theatre Design at Nottingham Trent Polytechnic. She is a visual artist and designer who has designed site specific and touring film and theatre works, and created installation artworks for unusual and digital spaces.

Janet has achieved particular recognition for her work as one third of mixed media experimentalists Talking Birds. Her design for Talking Birds' *Smoke, Mirrors & the Art of Escapology* formed part of the UK entry to the 1999 Prague Quadrennial, and *The Independent* has described her work with the company as "innovative and unusual...akin to taking part in a David Lynch movie." The main focus of Janet's theatre design is devised productions and new writing. Recent work includes: *Paradise* by Amber Lone (Birmingham Rep); *An Audience with Mr. Ritzy* by Nick Walker (Talking Birds); *Play to Win* by David Tse (Yellow Earth Theatre/Soho Theatre); *Wanderlust* and *Solid Blue* (both Talking Birds); she has also worked with The Belgrade Theatre, Triangle, Bare Essentials, Women & Theatre, C&T, mac and Stan's Cafe. More at www.vornster.co.uk

James Farncombe – Lighting Design

Theatre includes: *Blues for Mr Charlie* (Tricycle / New Wolsey, Ipswich); *Blest be the Tie* (Royal Court); *Playboy of the West Indies* Tricycle/ Nottingham Playhouse); *Forward* (Birmingham Rep); *The Maths Tutor* (Hampstead Theatre / Birmingham Rep); *West Side Story, To Kill a Mockingbird, Master Harold and the Boys, Death of a Salesman, Peter Pan, The Witches, Plague of Innocence, Unsuitable Girls* (Leicester Haymarket Theatre); *Beautiful Thing* (Nottingham Playhouse); *Urban Afro Saxons, Funny Black Women on the Edge* (Theatre Royal Stratford East); *This Lime Tree Bower* (Belgrade Theatre, Coventry); *Making Waves, Soap*; (Stephen Joseph Theatre, Scarborough); *The Hypochondriac, Dead Funny, Popcorn* (Bolton Octagon); *Amy's View* (Salisbury Playhouse / Royal Theatre, Northampton); *Krapp's Last Tape, A Different Way Home, A Visit from Prothero* (Lakeside Arts Centre, Nottingham); *Goldilocks* (Lyric Theatre Hammersmith); *The Blue Room, The Elephant Man* (Worcester Swan Theatre); *Mignon*; (Guildhall) *A Woman of No Importance, East Is East* (New Vic Theatre, Stoke); *Lord of the Flies, Bloodtide, Road, Rumblefish* (Pilot Theatre/York Theatre Royal). As assistant designer; *The Women in White* (West End).

Andy Garbi – Original soundscapes

Andy Garbi is one of the leading torchbearers for cross-genre music whose cutting edge composition and vocal work has gained the support of leading artists in all fields including the virtuoso Kennedy and Birmingham Royal Ballet director David Bintley. His reputation for composition is equally matched by his performances, the most recent of which (representing the UK for music at CBSO, Birmingham) earned him a commendation from the Royal Netherlands Embassy and the Arts Council of England. Andy has also made headline appearances at high calibre festivals across Europe, including Glastonbury and Terschelling's 'Oerol' (Netherlands) and has performed on the same bill as *the Prodigy*, *Roni Size*, *Trans Global Underground* and *Jah Wobble*. He formerly sang with legendary cult band 'Suns of Arqa' and co-founded the acclaimed group 'headhunters'. Andy won the Channel 4 Film Music Award *Ideasfactory* in 2004 and has just won a PRS Foundation ATOM award for advances in original music. As well as *Street Trilogy*, Andy has worked with Chris O'Connell on the plays *The Blue Zone* and most recently *Tall Phoenix*. *The Scotsman* described the music for *RAW* as 'extraordinary'.

Paul Simpson – Trainee Director

Paul has worked as an actor on all three plays in *Street Trilogy*, touring nationally and internationally. Paul has also worked extensively in film and TV. Paul is really happy to be working with Theatre Absolute and Mark Babych again. He would like to express his thanks to Theatre Absolute, Mark and the Arts Council of England for their continued support in his professional development. For Donna, Daisy and Harry.

Company

Stephen Cotton – Stage Manager

Stephen graduated in 2004 with a first class degree in Theatre and Performance Technology at the Liverpool Institute for Performing Arts. His previous experience includes work at the 2002 Manchester Commonwealth Games, the Lyceum Theatre at Crewe and the New Vic Theatre in Staffordshire. Stephen has recently returned from travelling around New Zealand managing various projects and product launches during his time abroad.

Will Evans – Technician and relights

Will trained at the Central School of Speech and Drama. Lighting design credits include *'Legend of Perseus'* (Big Wooden Horse Theatre), *'React!'* (Oscada productions), *'Spend Spend Spend'* and *'7 Lears'* (Birmingham School of Acting). Re-lights include a national tour of *'HMS Pinafore'* (Carl Rosa Opera), National Tour of *'Golden Boy'* (Broadway Productions), *'Something Else'* and *'Snow White'* (Tall Stories). Will is also on the executive of the Association of Lighting Designers, representing students. www.willevans.co.uk

Peter Ash – Nick (Car), Addy (Raw)

Peter studied at Xaverian College, Manchester. TV credits include: series regular on ITV's *Footballers Wives*, parts in *Casualty* and *Blue Murder*. Recent Film work includes the British independent film *Chicken Tikka Massala*.

Rachel Brogan – Lex (Raw)

Rachel has appeared at the Royal Court in *Redundant* and is a veteran performer at Manchester's Royal Exchange Theatre playing in *Port*, *The Sanctuary Lamp* and *Dog Boy*. Television appearances include *Casualty*, *Doctors* and *Spinechillers* for the BBC. She is also an experienced radio performer.

Sean Cernow – Marky (Car), K (Kid)

Sean completed his training at Salford University in 2000 and joined Contact Theatre's Young Actor's Company. Since then he has appeared in two feature films, Michael Winterbottom's *24 Hour Party People* and, most recently, Kenny Glennaan's *Yasmin*, a host of theatre productions including *Wise Guys* (Red Ladder) and the Channel 4 Prison Drama, *Buried*. As well as being an actor, Sean also writes plays, (the most recent piece, *Being Sebastian*, is to be shown in the autumn of 2005 at Salford Studios, Manchester), paints canvasses, plays guitar and writes songs and poetry which he performs around Manchester. Sean would like to dedicate his portrayals of 'K' and 'Marky' to his girlfriend, Saskia Evans.

Lee Colley – Jason (Car), Lee (Kid)

Lee's credits include *Murder of Stephen Lawrence* (Granada TV), *Band of Brothers* (HBO), *Red Cap*, *Cambridge Spies*, *Happiness*, *Final Demand* (BBC), *Serious and Organised*, *The Bill* (ITV). Lee has recently completed *Hiroshima* (BBC) portraying Captain van Kirk. Lee played Jason in the original award winning production of *Car* in 1999.

Belinda Everett – Shelley (Raw)

Belinda was born in Manchester. She trained at Salford College and London Academy of Music and Dramatic Art. Her credits include the British film *Calendar Girls*, *Holby City*, *Clocking Off*, *Cutting It* and *Playing the Field*. This is her first production for Theatre Absolute.

Daniel Harcourt – Tim (Car)

Daniel appeared in the original production of *Car*. He trained at Manchester University and the Welsh College of Music and Drama.
Theatre includes *Debris* (Latchmere Theatre); *Kes*, *Romeo and Juliet* and *Loot* (New Vic Stoke); *The Borrowers* (Library Theatre and Tour); *Macbeth* and *Romeo and Juliet* (English Shakespeare Co); *Another Country* (West End); *People On The River* (The Red Room); *Bonded* and *Bretevski St* (Birmingham Rep); *Hansel and Gretel* (Red Shift); *Angry Old Men* (Plymouth Theatre Royal); *Macbeth* (New End Theatre). TV and Film includes: *Grange Hill* (BBC); *Emmerdale*, *Number Ten* and *The Brief* (ITV).

Graeme Hawley – Gary (Car), Rueben (Raw)

Graeme's theatre credits include *Romeo and Juliet* (Eye); *Measure for Measure*, *Schweyk*, *Howie the Rookie* (Library Theatre, Manchester); *Hidden Markings*, *Traffic and Weather* (Homegrown Theatre); *Little Malcolm* (Octagon Theatre, Bolton). His TV credits includes *Emmerdale*, *The Royal*, *Cops*, *A & E*, *Strumpet*, *Touch of Frost*, *The Forsyte Saga*, *Born and Bred* and *Heartbeat*. Graeme has previously worked with Theatre Absolute on *Raw* and *Cloud: Burst*.

James Low – Robert (Car)

Theatre work includes Victor in *The Dice House* at the Belgrade Theatre, Coventry, and Birmingham Stage Company productions of the same play which performed at the Edinburgh Fringe Festival and in the West End at the Arts Theatre, London. Macduff in *Macbeth* at Worcester, Swan; Curly in *Of Mice and Men* at Southwark Playhouse. James has previously played Robert in *Car* which toured nationally across the UK and at the 'Londres Sur Scene' Festival , Paris.

Rebekah Manning – Lorna (Raw), Bradley (Kid)

Rebekah is delighted to be working with Theatre Absolute again after taking *Kid* to the Edinburgh Fringe Festival in 2003. She trained with the National Youth Theatre and at LAMDA. Her work includes *The BFG* at the Octagon Theatre, Bolton; *Eskimo Sisters* at the Pleasance Stage Space; *Foyles War*, *Doctors*, *A & E*, *Wire in the Blood*, *The Bill* and *Watch Over Me*. Rebekah would like to dedicate her performance to the memory of Ian Kenny, who would have loved Theatre Absolute's work.

Samantha Power – Trainers (Raw), Zoe (Kid)

Samantha trained at the Welsh College of Music and Drama. Theatre Credits include *Coming Around Again* and *Accrington Pals* for West Yorkshire Playhouse; *Little Malcolm and his Struggle Against the Eunuchs*, Octagon Theatre, Bolton; and *School Daze* at The Riverside Studios. TV credits include *Little Britain*, *Twisted Tales*, *The Royal*, *The Cops*, *City Central*, *The Low Down*. Samantha was involved in the original production of *Raw* and *Kid* and is delighted to be part of *Street Trilogy*.

STREET TRILOGY

First published in 2003 by Oberon Books Ltd
521 Caledonian Road, London N7 9RH
Tel: 020 7607 3637 / Fax: 020 7607 3629
e-mail: oberon.books@btconnect.com
www.oberonbooks.com

New edition (revised), 2005

A catalogue record for this book is available from the British
Library.

ISBN: 1 84002 389 9

Cover designed by Through and Through

Printed in Great Britain by Antony Rowe Ltd, Chippenham

Contents

Especially for Jo-Jo and Rube – thanks for understanding.

CAR

Characters

JASON
early twenties

NICK
nineteen

TIM
early twenties

MARKY
early twenties

GARY
thirties

ROBERT
forties

The present day. Summer.

The action unfolds over twenty-two days

The symbol / indicates an interruption point

Car was first performed by Theatre Absolute, in co-production with the Belgrade Theatre, on 22 June 1999, in Coventry's Transport Museum. The cast and production crew was as follows:

JASON,   Lee Colley

NICK,   Richard J Fletcher

MARKY,   Gary Cargill

TIM,   Daniel Harcourt

GARY,   Stephen Banks

ROBERT,   Mike Brogan

Director, Mark Babych

Set Design, Rachel Blues

Lighting Design, Wesley Hiscock

Stage Manager, Anna Shepherd

Producer, Julia Negus

The play transferred to the Pleasance Theatre for the 1999 Edinburgh Festival where the cast and crew remained the same except for Paul Bull, who re-lit the show. The play won a Scotsman Fringe First Award* at the Festival and after transferring to the Pleasance Theatre, London in the autumn, Car was awarded a Time Out Live Award – Best New Play on the London Fringe, 1999. In Spring 2000, Theatre Absolute re-mounted *Car* and toured extensively across the UK and to festivals in France, Germany and Ireland. The cast and crew were:

JASON, Simon Greiff (Craig Conway)

NICK, Paul Simpson

MARKY, Richard Oldham

TIM, Andres Salcedo

GARY, Jim Pyke

ROBERT, Jim Low (Michael Brophy)

Director, Mark Babych

Set Design, Rachel Blues

Lighting Design, Paul Bull

Stage Managers, Claudia Townsend / Gavin Taylor / John Greet

Producer, Julia Negus

* for outstanding new work

Scene 1

The twenty-third day of the month, twenty-two days after the car theft.

It is dark and there is rain, just the pouring of rain. There are four chairs on the stage. The four lads arrive, watch the 'car'. JASON runs his hand over it, from front to back. They wait, then they break in. There is the sound of the car starting and roaring away. Out of this comes GARY, screaming.

GARY: No!!!
    (*Through the next speech, the four boys stay in the car and make small, subtle movements that illustrate GARY's recollection of events. It's as if they are fractured pieces of his memory.*)
    I was running all the way up the street and it was
    pouring I mean I remember the rain on my face I
    watched the car go round the corner and I thought that
    was it like I'd never see it again one moment I'm sitting
    in the lounge we're settling down to watch the video and
    the next I'm out in the street and there's this feeling
    running through me like I'm made of sand like my life
    depends on getting that car back God knows why even
    now I can't work it out but they started coming back
    they were gesturing to me the lads in the car sticking
    their fingers up one was flashing his arse I'm thinking
    how hard I've worked to buy the bloody thing Melanie
    my wife she's screaming at me from the front 'get out of
    the way' I was scared daring them I was in the middle of
    the road and they were heading right for me the car sort
    of cruised by like they'd come really close rub it in and
    slip off again that's what they must've been up to there
    were two boys in the back slashing the seats then the car
    stalled and my hands were on the bonnet I was at the
    door there was a boy in the back pushing me in the face
    but I wasn't letting go I was holding onto one of the
    others and holding off the one with his hand in my face
    then the car started again it happened I mean they say

these things happen in slow motion don't they this didn't
I mean the car starts the boy in the back bites my finger
the door slams I fall over I stand up and they ram the
car into me head on that's how it was one two three bam
bam bam it put me up on the roof I'm wanting to kill
them I can't think of doing anything else and suddenly
the car's moving and I'm so fucking angry I'm really
going over the mark clinging on I'm car surfing down
the High Street one hundred two hundred and fifty yards
cut to pieces when you hit the ground like that you
decide that's it you decide you're about to die everything
you care about it seems useless and you feel like a blot
in the Universe there were all these feet you know in the
corner of my eye people passing by I must've looked
stupid lying there in my dressing gown I tried to get up
my legs were jelly and I fell forward blacked out bang
end of story.

(*Music plays and the boys de-construct the car.*)

Scene 2

*Twenty-two days previously. An hour after stealing the car. The
dialogue overlaps and should be fast and perfectly timed.*

NICK: Yeah so…?
JASON: So you don't wanna go round saying
NICK: So nothing, it was me, it was *me*…
TIM: You…?
NICK: Me.
MARK: Him ennit. / It was…
JASON: Him?
NICK: *I* got it, / I got in the driver's seat…
JASON: No, I got /
TIM: We all took the car /
MARK: …the car!!! See the fucker?
JASON: The owner?
MARK: He was / legging it…
JASON: Chasing us up the road /
TIM: …up the street.

NICK: He was crying, / did you see how he was crying...?
TIM: Real... /
JASON: ...there was real tears, / pouring out of him...
TIM: His car...
JASON: ...his car. And we're / we're...
TIM / MARK: We're.
  (*Beat.*)
NICK: We're...? *Just Me.* I'm off, / down the road...
TIM: No. We're.
NICK: Just me / you fucking idiots...
TIM: We're...
JASON: We're.
NICK: *Me.*
JASON: It was all / of us...
NICK: But *I'm* at the steering wheel.
JASON: All of us...
NICK: *I'm* at the steering wheel.
JASON: Me, Tim, / Marky.
NICK: I'm at the steering wheel.
TIM: No. It was a joint...
MARK: ...it was a joint effort ennit. Me, Jase, Tim...
NICK: So nothing, you don't understand.../ it was me...
JASON: All of...
TIM: Us.
MARK: All.
NICK: No. Me. / *I'm* at the steering wheel...
JASON: I'm changing gear...
TIM: And who did the...?
MARK: (*To TIM.*) You / did it.
TIM: Yeah. / Me.
NICK: But *I'm* at the / steering wheel...
JASON: The lock?
NICK: So *nothing.* It was down to *me...* Yeah, you're doing
    the gears...
TIM: ...and I did the lock, you / saying you did the lock as
    well...?
MARK: ...he didn't... (*To NICK.*) / you didn't do the lock...
NICK: I know I didn't, but *I'm* still at the steering wheel...
    I'm on the clutch, / I'm on the revs...

JASON: ...the clutch!! the clutch!! the revs!! the revs...
    Nicky Nicko we know / about the clutch!!...

NICK: You're not listening...

JASON: I am, we know, *I* know, the revs, the clutch, it's up,
    it's out and it's BANG! Away, you're away. We've all
    done it, we've all fucking done it, we've all been there,
    gripping the wheel, doing the steal. The speed, and the
    wind, the air vents open and the cold air whistling
    through the dash board. The vanished streets, lanky
    streetlamps and shadow cats, black fat cats, jumping
    clear, everyone's seen the dog leaping, fur shrieking,
    paws trembling. The car goes past, the speed on the
    meter the speed of a cheetah. It's me tonight and anyone
    tomorrow, it's up for grabs, you're picky Nicky, you're a
    spoiler, it's my night yeah? It's me and the car, set
    together, my eyes on the road, my smiles, my heart, my
    blood on the pulse, my steal. Prince Jase and the
    gormless dressing gown man on the hop, pursuing us,
    hoping, thinking he can see a clink, that somewhere
    there's some clink of a chance that the car's changing
    hands, going back to him and away from me. No. Not.
    Never.
    (*Pause.*)

NICK: But *I* was at the fucking *steering wheel!!*
    (*Silence. Then suddenly music plays and the boys dance,
    celebrate.*)

Scene 3

*Thirteen days previously. GARY's house. GARY supports himself with
a stick.*

GARY: ....does what I'm saying make sense?

ROB: Of course it does.

GARY: I've never had anything stolen in my life before
    when they stole my car I couldn't understand why I was
    behaving like I did. I know now, but I've never had any
    feelings like that before.

ROB: What sort of feelings?

GARY: Violent, like I could lose control.

ROB: Gary, bringing you face to face with this lad isn't going to lead to you murdering him if that's what you're worrying about. I'll do it for you. He's a frustrating little toe rag.

GARY: Is he?

ROB: I was being sarcastic... (*Beat.*) How're you doing anyway? Apart from feeling like you might kill someone.

GARY: It's not a joke.

ROB: I know it isn't. I wasn't joking.

GARY: Put yourself in my position, you're just sitting there, but it's me who's got to walk into this mediation thing you're talking about, it's me who's...

ROB: Gary, I deal with situations like this everyday, don't think I don't I understand how you feel. (*Beat.*) How's your injuries?

GARY: My back's covered in bruises I can hardly put any weight on my left leg my right hand shakes when I pour tea from the tea pot I've got a cut over my left eye and thick heavyweight plasters on both knees where I hit the tarmac apart from that I'm happy as a sandbag. (*Pause.*) Well?

ROB: I'm listening.

(*Pause.*)

GARY: So.

ROB: Well look, I'm not going to pressurise you. If you think getting together with this kid isn't the right thing, then fine, we'll leave it.

GARY: What does he want to do?

ROB: He wants to meet you. I've been through it with him. He knows he isn't going to get off with anything.

GARY: Why are you doing this? Sorry. Is this how you do things?

ROB: It's how *I* do things.

GARY: What does that mean?

ROB: I just believe, with something like this, that there's no point in the two of you sitting around going mad. You,

29

because you're angry, Nick because he's worrying. Why not bring the two of you together?

GARY: *You* believe it, no one else believes it because it sounds so crazy.

ROB: No. I believe it because I just... (*Beat.*) Trust me. (*Beat.*)

GARY: And I'm face to face with this lad?

ROB: Yeah. Give it some thought. There's no rush, he's still in police custody.

(*Beat.*)

GARY: What's his name?

(*ROB hesitates.*)

Come on, I'm not going to hunt him down, or anything. I just want to know. (*Beat.*) What's his name?

(*Beat.*)

ROB: Nick.

(*Lights change.*)

Scene 4

Still twenty-two days previously.

The four lads again.

JASON: ...sun roof, sun roof control switch, the same switch controls everything. Sun visor, positioned over either side window. Vanity mirror on the passenger's side, rear screen blinds. Glove box, oddment box, loose change box. Got loads of boxes. Cigarette lighter. Pushes in and springs back when it's ready to use. Ashtray. Interior lamps. Map reading lamp, swivels to the left and right. Hazard warning, rear wipers, rear screen wash, rear screen heating, electric windows, rear seat belts. Radio equipment. One loudspeaker in each front door, one loudspeaker in each rear quarter, or it's over the wheel arch in estates. Maximum power, two times twenty watts. Four wheel drive. Sixteen valve engine. Did I say that? Cubic capacity...fifteen eighty cc. Fuel tank capacity, fifty-two litres. Engine oil capacity, four point five litres drain. Five litres, nine pints drain and filter. Maximum speed, a hundred and five point six mph. Calculated. Main brakes, power operated. Tyres: front twenty-nine, rear twenty-nine, spare thirty-two. I nearly forgot, automatic gearbox.

(*Silence.*)

TIM: Did you learn all that?

JASON: Copy.

NICK: He knows his cars.

TIM: Boy genius.

(*JASON takes out a plastic bag full of bottles of pills. NICK sucks on his inhaler. MARK gets up.*)

TIM: Where you going?

MARK: Piss ennit. (*MARK goes.*)

JASON: You and Marky at it yeah?

TIM: What?

JASON: He's like your boyfriend or something, let him breathe.

TIM: You don't know him.

JASON: Don't mean he has to get permission for a piss. What you two plotting all the time? It's like you're a pair of plotters all the time.

TIM: You rob the chemists?

JASON: Sort of.

NICK: Fucking druggie.

JASON: I'm selling them yeah, don't take shit like this.

TIM: I'm off.

JASON: Nah.

TIM: Yeah, fuck this, got other things to do.

(*MARK returns.*)

JASON: Yeah, like shaking Marky's dick.

(*MARK grabs JASON and pulls him across the floor.*)

Get off!...fuck off...

TIM: Leave him.

(*MARK lays a kick into his side. NICK gets up and joins in. MARK stops, but NICK continues, not hard kicks, just niggly, provocative, kicking for the sake of being violent. JASON gets up and squares up to him.*)

JASON: You want to / go for it?

NICK: (*To JASON.*) Anytime.

TIM: No he doesn't...just leave it...

JASON: (*To NICK.*) What you taking it out on me for?

NICK: I ain't taking nothing out...

JASON: So what's all the edge for?

> (*Pause. NICK breaks away, takes the bag of pills, spills the bottles across the floor. JASON scrambles to pick them up and MARK kicks out at him, TIM pulling him back.*)

MARK: Junkie twat ennit.

JASON: Yeah.

MARK: Baghead.

TIM: You coming?

MARK: Might go to Louise's.

TIM: *What?* What you going there for?

MARK: Dunno...thought I might. Dunno.

> (*TIM heads for the door.*)

TIM: See yous... (*To MARK.*) Come on...

> (*TIM goes, MARK follows. Silence as NICK watches JASON who counts the pills again.*)

JASON: Seen these...? you seen all these...?

> (*No answer.*)

You talking or what?

> (*No answer. NICK lights up a ciggie.*)

Fucking noisy in here, yeah? Rats in the pipes. Fuck. Crickets, rats, coyotes, red backed antelopes, prime time horns, sniffing, sucking round the house, come back in the morning and there's a fucking dead antelope moved in. Yeah?

> (*No answer.*)

Fucking prime time company and stuff yeah? Nick – 'Entertainer' ...Nick – 'Laugh a Lot Man'. (*JASON turns to the pills again.*) Fuck this, can't wait, got to get on, got to get the counting going, copy? Two, three, four, six, eight, ten, fifteen yeah? Tidy price, do the dirty business and zoom, buy the motor, yeah? Seen it waiting, seen its seats waiting. Under the engine and you're like...

Whoosh! Motorway. Countryside. Wiltshire. Somerset... get down the corn fields, find the corn fields and get the corn circles going. Making a corn arse, that's the crack, that's the mission. I'd love it, I'd love to do it. I'd love to

leave this big fucking arse in the corn, and then
someone's flying over the field, and they look down and
they're all saying, 'Jesus! Look down there! It's an arse,
there's an arse in the corn!'

NICK: What dirty business?

(*JASON makes a 'gun' with his fingers, aims it at NICK.*)

JASON: S'not New York yeah...no way...but come Friday
I'm living it, yeah?...

NICK: What you on about?

(*JASON 'fires' the gun.*)

JASON: Puggggggggh!!! Merc. Ferrari. Three, four, six on
the drive. I'd love that, I'd fucking love that. I'd kill for
that yeah?

NICK: What planet you on?

JASON: Let's do another.

NICK: What?

JASON: Another car...

NICK: We just fucking did one.

JASON: So let's do another, I'm itching, I got the need... I
can do two, three, six, eight, ten, can't get enough...it's
just... I don't know...it's just... I don't know...it's just... I
don't know...it's just... I don't know...it's just... I don't
know...it's just... I don't know...it's just... I don't
know...it's just... I don't know...it's just... I don't
know...it's just... I don't know...it's just... I don't
know...it's just the *shape*, the feel, the speed yeah? It's
what I want one day, I want to settle down with a wife
and kids and things. I want a family and I want a car,
you know what I mean? But I want one of the best, not
some shitty thing we went out robbing tonight.

NICK: That was all too hot by the way, too risky.

JASON: We still got the car though yeah?

NICK: I said we should leave it, you could see the curtains
twitching all over the shop...

JASON: Don't get something for nothing.

NICK: Yeah, but I don't want to wake up in some pig
station. I'm not going in some cell, can't breath in a
fucking cell.

JASON: When's the last time you ever went in a cell, any fucking cell yeah?

NICK: One, two years.

JASON: Time you paid a visit.

NICK: Kids.

JASON: Who?

NICK: Us. My cousin talks like you, he says goo, goo, gaa, gaa. He's eighteen months old and he talks better than the lot of us put together.

JASON: No. Not your cousin. Can he walk?

NICK: Yeah.

JASON: Does he drive?

NICK: Has to use those big wooden blocks to reach the pedals.
(*Beat.*)

JASON: I'd like to meet your cousin.

NICK: Whenever. You coming...?

JASON: Copy.
(*NICK exits ahead of JASON. JASON follows and stops as his mobile rings.*)
Yeah? alright. Yeah?...prime time...yeah I am, I'm listening... I'm listening, just tell me. (*He listens.*) Seven-thirty? In the Crown. Yeah. Okay. Copy.
(*He rings off.*
Music plays.)

Scene 5

TIM's flat. Twenty-one days previously. The day after the car theft.

Music plays. TIM stands in a light. He has a razor, looks at the blade, waits, stares at himself in the mirror. MARK sits with a cardboard box, inside: milk, bread, tins, tea, cereal.

MARK: What about the milk? Tim?

TIM: Chuck it.

MARK: Margarine...what about the bread?

TIM: Bin it.

MARK: The bread?

TIM: What do you think? Will you want any more toast? Any more milky drinks?

MARK: Fuck off.

TIM: So bin it.

MARK: If I just knew when. If you'd say, then I could know ennit...

TIM: I will.

MARK: Today. Tonight. Tomorrow. If it's tomorrow maybe I'll be wanting to eat again.

TIM: What you on about, you've eaten nothing today. A bowl of corn flakes, that's not even eating to begin with.

MARK: I need to know ennit.

TIM: 'I need to know ennit...'

(*MARK chucks the milk carton at the wall, grabs the breakfast stuff, cereal box, sugar, cereal bowl, shoving them into the bin. TIM comes to his side, pulls him back by the shoulders so they face each other. MARK backs away.*)

MARK: Sorry...

(*TIM grabs him by the wrists.*)

Fuck off...

(*TIM gets MARK by the throat. They struggle, but it is MARK who begins to get the better of TIM until eventually he holds him in a headlock. There is a silence and only the sound of TIM gasping for breath.*)

TIM: Marky...

(*MARK forces TIM to his knees and lets him go, turning to kick the shit out of the bin. Finally, MARK calms and they wait in silence.*)

MARK: Sorry...

(*Long silence.*)

...couldn't sleep last night... Feeling so shitty.

TIM: Shut it.

MARK: Yeah.

TIM: No I mean it, we're gonna solve it.

MARK: Yeah.

(*Silence.*)

I've writ a note.

TIM: We don't need it.

MARK: What?

(*Beat.*)

Did you get any ideas...for doing it...?

TIM: Some.

MARK: What sort?

TIM: The motor we nicked last night, Jason's still got it.

MARK: Yeah?

TIM: We'll use that.

MARK: You sure we're doing the right thing?

TIM: Christ, how do you feel, what were you saying just now?

MARK: I know.

TIM: What were you saying?

MARK: That I feel... I feel...

TIM: We made a pact.

MARK: Your idea ennit.

TIM: You agreed.

MARK: Yeah. But I'm just thinking, you know, when are we gonna actually...

TIM: Soon.

MARK: Yeah. So what do we do until then. Now. While we're waiting.

TIM: Pass the time. I don't know. *Am I sure we're doing the right thing?* What the fuck do you think? How long you been feeling the way you feel now?

(*No answer.*)

TIM: How long?

MARK: Dunno...

TIM: How long?

MARK: It / doesn't matter.

TIM: Come on, how long...

MARK: I told you...

TIM: Like did you get upset suddenly cos you realised you can't stop stealing people's fucking cars...

MARK: What...?

TIM: Why'd you agree?

MARK: Agree?

TIM: To the pact.

MARK: What the fuck're you talking about...?

TIM: How long?

(*No answer.*)

How long?

MARK: What the fuck're are you talking about...?

TIM: How long.

MARK: What the fuck are you going on about...?

TIM: How long, / how long...

MARK: *What!?*

TIM: How long? how long...?

MARK: Will you / fuckin shit it ennit...

TIM: How long?

(*MARK explodes, pushes TIM back across the room, one push, two, three, advancing on TIM, TIM standing his ground.*)

MARK: ...how long how long how long how long how long *fucking what...?*

(*Silence.*)

(*Quieter.*) ...since I felt like... (*Running out of steam.*) ...all my life...all my fucking...

(*Silence. MARK sits. TIM gets a hand held Nintendo game. He plays in the silence, and the sound of the game echoes around the room. NICK arrives.*)

NICK: Alright? ...Anyone got a ciggie?

(*He takes the one MARK has just put in his mouth.*)

Got a wicked fucking hangover. What you up to?

TIM: What's it look like?

NICK: Breakfast. Listen...

MARK: What?

NICK: That guy last night, d'you reckon he's okay, did he get up when we dumped him in the street?

TIM: Don't know.

NICK: Me neither. (*Beat.*) Jase came round last night, three in the morning, he's going down to Somerset.

MARK: Why?

NICK: Don't know.

TIM: Did he take the car?

NICK: Can't walk to Somerset. Fucking wild last night.

MARK: See the fucker on the roof!

TIM: (*To MARK.*) You think that's cool?

MARK: No.

NICK: I was worrying.

TIM: Why?

NICK: That guy on the roof. Before it's always been dead easy and that, no one's ever chased us. I was looking at my lips, look... (*He shows them his lower lip.*) all chewed, didn't know I was... I got carried away.

TIM: Oh that's alright then, the pigs'll probably let you off then, yeah?

NICK: What? Get fucked. That guy might've croaked it? We nicked his car, but I don't want to waste my life in the jail cos of some stolen fucking car.

TIM: Your life.

(*Beat.*)

NICK: What's that mean?

TIM: Nothing.

NICK: So what's with the smirking?

TIM: I'm not smirking.

NICK: Fucking college boy. You want to get yourself back down the Student's Union...

TIM: I left. I told you.

NICK: Go and do your smirking down there, yeah? What the fuck's going on with you? You're getting colder every fucking day I look at you. You're ice.

(*Silence.*)

MARK: So when's Jase coming back?

NICK: Never with a bit of luck.

TIM: You got his mobile number?

(*Music plays. NICK hands over a scrap of paper that TIM dials from.*)

Scene 6

Twenty-one days previously. A field in Somerset.

Music plays throughout. In the field, JASON approaches, swinging a gun in his hand like a scythe, chopping through the corn. His mobile rings.

JASON: Yeah...?

(*TIM speaks on the other end of the phone.*)

TIM: Alright? Where are you?

JASON: Somerset...dunno.

TIM: What you doing?

JASON: I'm gardening. I'm making an arse. I'm standing in
a corn field and I'm expecting some ruby red face farmer
to come and shoot me with his hunting gun.

TIM: You're making the shape of an arse in a corn field?

JASON: Copy.

TIM: Why?

JASON: This way the Jumbos flying past get it in the teeth,
beedy eyed passengers pressing their conks against the
windows, smeary glass smeary with snot and spit, people
in a million years, looking and muttering as the Jumbo
grumbles past: 'we give in, we can see, now we
understand what it means: 'Jase woz ere!''

TIM: Nutter.

JASON: So what's the situation? I'm busy.

TIM: Can you bring the car back for us? I want it.

JASON: Go out and nick some other fucker's.

TIM: I want that one.

JASON: Whatever. Got to come back anyhows, got some
business to take care of. I'm doing my arse and then I'm
out of here.

TIM: Drop the car round.

JASON: Nice talking to you.

(*JASON hangs up.*)

MARK: Is he bringing the car back?

TIM: Said he was.

NICK: I'm off anyhows.

MARK: What did you come round for?

NICK: Dunno. (*Sees the cigarette in his hand.*) Ciggie.

(*Music plays.*)

Scene 7

ROBERT's office. Fifteen days previously.

NICK sits in the same position as in the last scene, but now faces

39

ROBERT and stirs from deep in thought as if he has been remembering the scene just played.

NICK: ...what?...

ROB: I said...

NICK: What?

ROB: I said, 'it's always nice to see you, but is this just a social visit cos there's no one else to knock around with, or did you come up to see me for a specific reason?'
(*No answer.*)

ROB: So what's up?

NICK: Nothing.
(*ROBERT waits.*)

NICK: What?

ROB: I'm waiting.

NICK: Don't look at your watch, yeah?

ROB: I'm not. I just wasn't expecting you, it's not a supervision day is it?
(*Pause.*)

ROB: You in the shit again?

NICK: Something like that.
(*ROBERT sighs.*)

NICK: That's exactly why I wasn't going to come.

ROB: What is?

NICK: That, you sighing, acting like I'm some fucking useless.../

ROB: Well what did you think I was going to say? You've been told enough times haven't you, you know what is and what isn't against the law.

NICK: I know that yeah, you don't need to go on and stuff.

ROB: So what happened?

NICK: Don't know. Just one of them.
(*Beat.*)

ROB: Look, I was sighing cos I wish you'd just come up here and pass the time of day or something, but it's always got to be when you've gone and fucked up somewhere.

NICK: You're swearing now, yeah?
(*ROBERT glares at him. Softens.*)

ROB: I'm just pissed off....You've been doing alright. So
    what is it, what you been up to?

NICK: I didn't mean it, yeah?
    (*Beat.*)

ROB: Didn't mean what? (*No answer*) Didn't mean *what?*

NICK: ...Me and these others...we robbed this bloke's car.
    Most times stuff like that goes in one ear and out the
    other. But then there's this car, and everything gets
    fucked up...The bloke starts chasing us and he ends up
    on the roof...he's smashed up on the road and the other
    guys, they just...and I'm fucking... It's doing my head
    in, going round, night time, day time, what we did to
    that guy...and it's like, how bad do I get, yeah?

ROB: Bad?

NICK: All the years, all the badness I'm storing up and now
    it's coming out.

ROB: Nick, you've been an idiot, / you've done some stupid
    things, but...

NICK: I know what I'm like yeah, fucking dam builder,
    man.
    (*Pause.*)

ROB: You could get sent down for this.

NICK: Got to hand myself in first.

ROB: Well don't start thinking it's going to go / away.

NICK: Yeah.

ROB: How badly hurt was this guy?

NICK: Didn't stop to look.

ROB: Sarcasm isn't going to get you anywhere. Who was
    he?

NICK: I just said.

ROB: Well what street was it? What area were you in?

NICK: Forget.

ROB: So think.

NICK: You need to help me man.

ROB: I need to lock you up and throw away the fucking
    key.

NICK: They're going to do that anyway!

ROB: Yeah, if they've got any sense they will. Did you tell anyone else yet?

NICK: No.

ROB: Your mum?

NICK: I can't talk to her.

ROB: So start trying. (*Laughing, incredulous.*) Go and tell your mum what you just told me.

NICK: Fuck off!! Don't joke with me!...don't fucking...I'm not...

(*NICK is hardly able to speak. He gets his breath, wipes his eyes.*)

NICK: The guy might've died for fucks sake.

(*Pause.*)

ROB: What if you were able to meet up with him?

NICK: Who?

ROB: The bloke whose motor you nicked. (*NICK looks at ROBERT like he's just farted.*) It's just a thought.

NICK: So try another one, yeah?

ROB: Mediation. Bringing the victim and the offender together.

NICK: How? / Says who?

ROB: I'll arrange it.

NICK: Meet him?

ROB: Yeah.

NICK: *Fucking meet him?!!* You mean like in court?

ROB: No. Face to face. Private. See what he's feeling, see the effect you've had on him. You'll be able to say sorry to him. Sounds to me that's what you're after.

NICK: So he didn't die then?

ROB: How do I know? Did you check the hospitals?

NICK: No.

ROB: Listen, if you do this.../

NICK: Do what? / I don't know what the fuck all this mediation shit is...

ROB: You need to listen to me.

NICK: You're moving too fast.

ROB: That's me Nick. Always a step ahead. Yeah? You want me to help, this is the way we do things. (*Beat.*) If this

guy agrees to meet you, then you've got to use it, do you
know what I'm saying? Either you let the system make
the choices for you: you go to jail, you come back out,
you sign on for a month, and then you fuck up again. Or
you can do this, and you can help yourself make the
switch. You're running out of time, every time you let
people down, every time you let me down...

NICK: You? How am I letting you down? I don't owe you
nothing. (*NICK sees ROBERT's look.*) You think we're
mates, or something?

(*Beat.*)

ROB: No.

NICK: No, you're my probation officer, yeah?

(*Silence. ROB gets busy, papers, pens etc.*)

ROB: Right, well whatever you decide to do, I'll do what I
can to help. Alright?

NICK: You telling me to go?

ROB: Yeah. Seems like you've got the situation sussed, I'm
sure you'll sort something out.

NICK: Rob, fuck's sake, you're acting like you're my
missus or something.... Are we having a row, yeah?
Don't blank me man!

ROB: Do you think I'm sitting here for the good of my own
health?

NICK: Dunno.

ROB: Don't be a smart arse! You want me to help you, then
alright, I'll give you a hundred per cent. But if you start
fucking me about / then...

NICK: It's pressure, fucking pressure all the time...I don't
want to keep fucking things up...Listen, tell me what this
mediation shit's about then, you think it's going to help
me?

ROB: You need to listen to what I tell you.

NICK: I am...I will...

ROB: First things first, you better go and hand yourself in.

Scene 8

Eighteen days previously. TIM's flat.

JASON, TIM and MARK. Frenzy! Music plays.

JASON, holding a gun, pants uncontrollably. The other two watch him as he moves around the kitchen. They track him, anticipating his drop to the floor at any moment. JASON moving, and the other two with arms out ready to catch him. All the time, JASON points the gun.

JASON: See...see...see, see, see, see? See, see, see...the barrel...see the smoke, see...see...see...see...see...see... (*He continues 'see...see' underneath the dialogue.*)
MARK: Give me the gun...give me the gun...
JASON: See...see...see...
MARK: Get ready to catch him.
JASON: See...see...see...
MARK: Give me the gun... Jase...give me the gun... (*JASON suddenly waves the gun around. The other two hit the deck. It doesn't fire, and the circling continues.*)
JASON: See...see...see...see...
TIM: *See fucking what?*
JASON: See, see, see...
TIM: Shut the fuck up or get out yeah?
JASON: No, not out, stay here...come on... I'm sweating, I'm shaking, and I'm carrying the metal, smell the blood on the shadow of the bullet. Bullet travels fast, leaves a phantom... Can you see it...? (*Silence. They are all looking at the end of the gun. JASON continues 'see...see' under the dialogue.*)
TIM: Who did you shoot?
JASON: I just did the job and I left.
MARK: Get rid of it.
TIM: Jase. Jason. We're taking the gun.
JASON: Take it and sling it, that's what *they* said.
TIM: Why the fuck'd you come here?
JASON: You told me to come back. I had to come back. I had a job to do.

MARK: The car.

JASON: Yeah, it's outside.

TIM: Give me the keys.

JASON: The car?...

TIM: Jase.

JASON: The car?

TIM: Jase...

JASON: The car? the car, the car, the car, the car, the car, the car, the car, the car, the car, I noticed...it's red. My old man, he drives a red car. He's always driven red cars. In Japan, so he tells me, they drive white cars. Drive red cars and you're not trustworthy. My dad travels abroad and he always comes back with presents for me and my sister and he kisses my mum like he's missed her, like he's really missed her, and then he kisses me and my sister, he gets tears in his eyes and they glisten, you know when mercury breaks out of a thermometer, like it's had too much telling to do and it sends its drops, one, two, three, four, solid drops down to the floor. My dad's tears; like a mercury drop. And we're all happy to be together. We're a family on a beach, holding hands and sharing jokes. My dad tells a joke and I look up at him, I like the way his face spreads when he smiles. In my head, I'm on the beach a million times a day and the happiness gets infectious. I'm desperate for it. Beach life; give me that happy life on the beach. But then in the Crown tonight, pulling the trigger, the beach falls in and my whole life pours into the egg timer hole left gaping in the crust of the earth. Everything's changed, forever.

(*JASON sinks to the floor. The other two watch, lulled by his speech.*)

TIM: You alright?

JASON: Feel sick.

TIM: You've just murdered someone.

(*JASON begins to crack. MARK puts a hand on him, JASON holds onto MARK and the tears come pouring out.*)

JASON: What do I do? Tell me what to do.

TIM: You did it yeah?

JASON: Just me.

TIM: Where? Who?

JASON: A lad, I knew him from my school. He said, 'No, please.'

MARK: Who sent you? Why did they send you to kill him? Why did you have to kill him?

JASON: Money...too much to talk about. They told me his name, told me where he'd be, like they'd had him watched.

MARK: Do they sell you your drugs...? They sell you your drugs ennit...

JASON: Fucking copy, now they bought my soul, now they bought my fucking life.

(*JASON weeps and MARK holds him. TIM stands.*)

TIM: You'll have to sort yourself out Jase.

JASON: What?

MARK: Tim?

TIM: We're not getting involved.

MARK: He'll have the pigs after him.

TIM: No.

JASON: You're supposed to be my mates.

TIM: Not this time.

MARK: We can't just / leave him.

TIM: We've got our own stuff to think about.

JASON: I'm not asking much.

TIM: Wash the blood off your clothes, bury the gun, give you an alibi, and stand up in court and lie for you.

JASON: Would that be alright yeah?

MARK: I'll get rid of the gun.

TIM: No.

JASON: (*Of MARK.*) Let him breathe, yeah?

TIM: Marky, we're not getting involved.

MARK: I want to help him.

JASON: I'll buy you both a pint.

TIM: I said no.

JASON: Two pints.

MARK: Don't act like you're my old man. I'll do it for him cos we're mates, we're all mates.

JASON: Two pints and a packet of Ready Salted.

TIM: We steal cars together, we don't go any deeper, there's nothing else between any of us.

JASON: Each.

MARK: So now you're telling me no one's my friend, you're saying there's no one I can call my friend ennit.

JASON: I'm your friend.

TIM: (*To JASON.*) Any petrol left in the car?

JASON: Where you going?

TIM: Down the coast.

JASON: The other day...

TIM: What?

JASON: Went Nick's. Not there... Mumma Nick, nice woman, lips to suck the life out, said he's going to confess, get himself bailed.

TIM: He wouldn't grass on us.

JASON: Who gives a fuck anyway?

MARK: Not you.

JASON: Listen... I'd really like it if you could help me. Prime time and that, get me sorted. Yeah?... I've got to hide away for a bit, I'm a major suspect... What am I gonna do eh?!! Please... I NEED SOME HELP!!! (*Music plays.*)

Scene 9

Seven days previously. Two weeks after the car theft.

GARY's house. GARY alone.

GARY: I'm in the bath and the phone rings I can hear the phone ringing and Melanie's out for the night and I know the answering machine's not on so I'm out of the bath and I'm dripping across the landing to the bedroom where I answer the phone and Robert says he hopes he didn't disturb me and I laugh and say of course he didn't and inside I know what he's about to ask me how he's following up this mediation thing he mentioned before it's been in his head and it's been in mine every minute every day and it's going to be his question like I knew it would be and inside I know I'll say yes I'll do but just as

I swap hands and put the receiver in my other hand I'm feeling weak like my legs are going to give way because I suddenly think will this mediation stuff make me feel better or worse and it's going round and round my head again how it's not fair how this has happened to me and I'm getting this sort of phone call and this sort of pressure and how the bubble's burst around me and the world's pouring in but I hear myself speaking and I'm telling Robert I'll do it I'll go and meet the lad because I'm a good bloke and I want to be a man and do what a person needs to do and I make him understand it's not just for me it's for everyone who ever got anything nicked and I tell Melanie when she gets in and I've still got the wet towel round me and she says I'll feel better for it. (*He stops.*) So. I'm trying not to think about it… (*Beat.*) I've been trying not to think about it. (*Music plays.*)

Scene 10

Ten days previously. In the street.

JASON stands with his foot on NICK's head. NICK is on the floor.

JASON: …alright, so how long've you known me?

NICK: What's that got to do with anything?

JASON: You were trying to work out if I was going to let you go or squash your brains out yeah?

NICK: Something like that.

JASON: And I said, 'Don't you trust me…?'

NICK: Yeah.

JASON: You do?

NICK: I dunno.

JASON: So you've known me since school yeah, and I was always dead fair and that at school, yeah?

NICK: I dunno, I didn't have much to do with you back then…

JASON: Think.

NICK: From what I heard you were, yeah.

JASON: Copy. I was. So, you can get up in a minute, after we've sorted it out for the twenty-third...

NICK: The twenty-third?

JASON: Now, you can go in there and tell all your fucking stories about the car and that.

NICK: What car?

JASON: I'm not daft. Squealing like a pig, getting yourself off the hook yeah?

(*He hauls NICK to his feet.*)

NICK: I won't get off the hook...

JASON: No? So what's this shit your old lady says you're doing ten am, *sharp*, teeth washed, balls brushed, on the twenty-third, with your probation officer?

NICK: She told you about that?!

JASON: Copy. And you wouldn't say nothing to grass on no one would you?

NICK: No.

JASON: Bullshit, you ain't no angel. I seen what you carry in your pockets.

NICK: But I still wouldn't grass on no one.

JASON: Yeah? But that's my point, you can *tell* the fuckers I was involved in stealing that poxy Golf. Tell them, I don't care that I did it. You get second rate cars, they fall off the track, false fucking interiors, they're not real cars. Real cars are privileged cars. Only those that are allowed drive those sort of cars, and that's the sort of car I wouldn't take no rap for. That's the sort of car I'm driving myself, yeah?

NICK: Are you?

JASON: Soon I will be. So tell them about the poxy Golf, just don't tell them anything else...

NICK: I won't say nothing.

JASON: Don't say nothing about the drugs and the shooting I was involved in...

NICK: The...?

JASON: You tell them I killed that lanky lad / and I'll be...

NICK: You what...??!! Who the fuck did you kill?!!

JASON: *You shouting at me yeah?!*

NICK: Let me up!!...who the fuck did you kill?

(*JASON pulls out the gun and pursues NICK, as NICK backs away.*)

Jesus, fuck... I didn't know you killed anyone... when?...

JASON: Last Friday.

NICK: Let me get out of your fucking sight man. I don't want nothing to do with no killer, you're nothing to do with me, Jesus, the pigs come and they lift *you* and I get. / Fuck...

JASON: It's cool, they can't catch me...

NICK: You gone too far this time... Put it away. Jase. / Jase!!...

JASON: Just don't say nothing.

NICK: I won't, I don't know nothing about no killing.

JASON: So I'm telling you now. Don't go squealing.

NICK: I wouldn't...

JASON: Well don't.

NICK: I won't.

(*Silence.*)

JASON: I've got to hide away, I'm keeping out the area till it all blows over. I'm a major suspect, don't go squealing...

NICK: Who did you kill?

(*JASON thrusts the gun back into NICK's face.*)

JASON: There you go, you're squealing already!

NICK: *I'm not! I'm not! You fucking brought the subject up man!!*

(*Pause. JASON puts the gun back in his pocket.*)

You're a nutter.

JASON: And you've got my footprint on your head. Copy?

(*Music plays.*)

Scene 11

Thirteen days ago. TIM's flat.

MARK has a hosepipe around his neck, he throttles himself, pushes it as far as he dare until he drops back, freeing the hose, gasping for air.

TIM comes in, drinking from a can.

MARK: Fucking hot yeah?

(*No answer. TIM screws up the can, chucks it by the bin.*)
Pisshead.

TIM: What's that for?

(*MARK indicates the tap attachment on the end of the hosepipe.*)

MARK: Get this bit off and...

(*He makes an upward movement.*)

TIM: And what?

MARK: Up the exhaust.

TIM: No.

MARK: What then?

(*No answer. Silence.*)

I was...

(*He stops.*)

TIM: What?

MARK: I was gonna go back tonight, see / Louise...

TIM: No.

MARK: Yeah. See her, the kids. It'll be...like I won't see them again. They're my kids.

TIM: No.

MARK: Just for a bit ennit.

TIM: You won't come back.

MARK: I will, she's thrown me out yeah?

TIM: Yeah, so you'll try and get her to take you back.

MARK: No.

TIM: Yeah. She's not interested, she doesn't want you.

MARK: She said...she just says I'm a wanker ennit / she didn't say...

TIM: She's fed up with you beating the shit out of her.

MARK: Don't fucking start ennit.

TIM: I'm not, I'm trying to make you see. You've been *banned* from the estate.

MARK: Yeah. But it's my rights to go where I want.

TIM: People don't want you down there, they're frightened of you. They don't want you because you're too fucking violent. Fuck, your own kids're scared of you. You see Louise just once and / you'll be fucking...

MARK: I won't.

TIM: You can't control yourself.

MARK: You're not my social worker, yeah?

TIM: Marky, I'm your mate, I know you, I know your old man.

MARK: I'm not like that fucker ennit.

TIM: No?

MARK: What you trying to do to me...?

TIM: Me?

MARK: What you doing...

TIM: I'm not doing anything...

MARK: *Yeah...* Fucking with my head.

TIM: Me?

MARK: ...telling me, all the time...*telling* me what to think...

(*Silence.*)

The other day...

TIM: What about it?

MARK: I hugged Jason, he was crying and he didn't have anyone else to turn to.

TIM: Neither did the poor bastard / who got the bullet.

MARK: But I'm saying!!... I'm trying to *tell* you, I've got something, there's something...more... Fuck, I didn't mean to do it, but he was crying and I just hugged him ennit. I want to go and give the kids a present and kiss Louise goodbye.

TIM: Look...listen yeah? See it from my point of view. Everyday you're leeching it. Fucking leech man everyday. I *know* what you think, I don't need you going on all the time. All the years, all the fucking times we've done things your way, and where's it got us? Nowhere. Now it's my turn, now we do things how I say. 'I feel so shitty.' I know you do, so I'm going to solve it, but now you're running back to Louise and your kids. I mean, either we do, or we don't. Do you want to spend the rest of your life in this fucking place? Do you want to hang around with nutters like Jason all your life? People hating you all the time. Is that what you want to do? (*Long silence. TIM waits.*)

MARK: No.

TIM: We'll take the car down the coast.

MARK: Yeah.

TIM: Where's the booze I bought last night?

MARK: Bottom of the bin.

TIM: Why?! Just let me drink what I want alright?

(*TIM goes to the bin and starts to rummage through the contents. He finds the booze, swigs from it. MARK looks at a note he takes from his pocket. TIM gets two black bin liners and starts to fill them.*)

MARK: What you doing?

TIM: We take these, and we put them in the boot of the car.

MARK: Books...cheque stubs, dole card, rent book... You chucking all this out? (*He takes out some books.*) You read these?

TIM: Some.

MARK: College shite.

TIM: Just things I bought. I tried reading them.

(*NICK arrives.*)

NICK: Alright?

(*MARK goes for him, shoves him against the wall.*)

MARK: What the fuck *you* doing here, *fucking grass*...

NICK: No.

MARK: *Yeah*, Jase told us what you was doing, going down the Feds, getting yourself bailed.

TIM: He won't say nothing.

MARK: So what's he doing it for?

NICK: I'm not grassing on no one, yeah? It's just stuff I'm doing with my probation officer...it's alright.

MARK: I'm fucking watching you.

(*Long silence.*)

NICK: What yous up to?

TIM: I was explaining to Marky. (*Beat.*) You can help with something.

(*TIM gets a digital video camera.*)

NICK: Yeah? Help with what? (*Seeing the video.*) Where'd you nick that...!

TIM: (*To MARK.*) Sit.

(*MARK sits on a chair.*)

Over here, with me.

MARK: Oooh, over there with you.

NICK: Fucking porno movies!

MARK: Fuck off you queg.

(*MARK and TIM face NICK who has the video.*)

TIM: (*To NICK.*) Press record yeah?

NICK: What?

TIM: The red button.

NICK: I know what fucking 'record' looks like... (*Fumbles for the button.*) What you up to?

TIM: (*To MARK.*) Say something.

MARK: Like what?

TIM: Get your note, read it out.

MARK: I chucked it.

TIM: Find it.

(*MARK gets up, flashes his arse at the camera. He and NICK are laughing.*)

Leave it, just keep it recording.

(*NICK returns the camera to its original point. TIM focuses on the camera. The whole of this next section should be as humorous as it is 'serious', with many opportunities for MARK and NICK to perform for the camera, playing against the tension of TIM's dialogue.*)

Can you see me?... Should be able to... Testing. It's Wednesday.

(*Blackout. The lights rise and MARK is still over by the bin. NICK is behind the camera, non-plussed. TIM speaks to the camera.*)

...At the start I'm just a kid...easy to fall in line... See the line, all you can see's the line.

(*Blackout. The lights rise.*)

Fuck. I don't know, I could say a million things ... Like, you get the landlord wanting his money and you tell him you really want to pay, you tell him you really want to keep the place... You feel like you're getting on, a decent conversation between two people, that's all you want, and then he's banging your fucking door down, wants his cash...but I've got to drink That's the stage. That's the situation. And it's like...I stay the same. Nothing shifts, and you get feelings...yeah? You don't fit, you don't want what people want to give you. But I don't want *this*, what I've got. Boredom. That's what I've been telling myself, I'm getting ignorant, more and more.

NICK: Anyone got a spare ciggie...?

(*Blackout. The lights come straight back up. MARK is now just off TIM's shoulder, moving into the frame of the camera. NICK has taken a seat.*)

TIM: ...What was I saying...?

NICK: What this all about then? What's the crack jack?

TIM: (*To the camera.*) ...it's like with Marky... He's down there, in the pits...but how's he understand, how's he know himself enough to get back up, to get the strength?

NICK: Fucking nutty.

TIM: I've got the brains to help him, got the brains to help myself, but things get wasted, and then you realise... you're no good to anyone.

NICK: I'm off then yeah?

(*NICK and MARK crack up laughing.*)

TIM: ...burglary...assault...nicking cars... Marky leads and I just follow. Next time it's the jail, no way, not the cell, not the smell...

(*Blackout. Lights up.*)

Look in the mirror, and hate what you see...

(*Blackout. The lights come back up. TIM sits alone. MARK looks at the camera, licks his lips, spreads his legs. They are in porno movie mode. NICK 'rings' the bell.*)

NICK: Bing bong.

MARK: (*Swedish sex siren.*) Who is it?

NICK: (*German porno star.*) My name is Helmut. I've come to fix the plumbing.

(*They are all laughing now.*)

MARK: (*Stroking between his legs.*) Oh, Helmut... Have you come to fixa my pipes...?

NICK: Yes.

MARK: Oooh yes, yes, come and-a-fixa my fuff Helmut.

(*NICK shoves the camera between MARK's legs. Much laughter as he and NICK simulate sex with the camera, until MARK lets rip with a huge farting noise.*)

TIM: Mark, you smelly bastard! Blowing off in front of the camera!

(*MARK does another.*)

Oh Christ, he's at it again...

(*TIM joins in. Farting noises left right and centre, they begin to play to the camera, like kids showing off to their parents. NICK is laughing with them, getting drawn into them and starts to make noises too. TIM puts his face against the camera lens, MARK speaks in silly voices. They stick their fingers up to the camera, shouting, gesticulating. MARK bares his arse to the camera. The farting noises continue and they crack up, laughing at themselves, fanning away the fumes. NICK goes into overdrive, overacting, more and more exaggerated, crying out.*)

NICK: No...fuck...you're killing me... (*He grabs his throat, falling to the floor, melodramatic suffocation.*) ...I can't breathe...you're killing me...aaaah!!!...you're fucking killing me...

(*MARK and TIM stop, their laughter fading as they realise the sense of NICK's overacted irony. NICK lies on the floor, still laughing to himself.*)

Scene 12

Music plays. NICK takes a letter from an envelope, reading it as if for the first time. MARK takes an envelope, the same one effectively, from his pocket, and looks at it.

Lights fade.

Scene 13

The present. Twenty-two days previously.

The mediation room. GARY stands at the window. He has a stick for support.

ROBERT enters. Pause.

ROB: Alright?

GARY: I'm trying to stay calm is he in the building is he here now…?

ROB: Yes. Now. Gary, simple facts; if you can't stay calm, then we'll just have to postpone today and wait until you're in a better frame of mind.

GARY: I'm ready.

ROB: For what?

GARY: To meet him.

ROB: And are you ready to talk?

GARY: Don't look at me like that I'm the one who had his car nicked I'm the one who ended up lying in the street.

ROB: Fine.

(*Silence. GARY loosens his tie.*)

GARY: I can't believe this heat.

(*GARY is at the window.*)

Is that a fire over there?

ROB: Where?

GARY: Can you see, where the ring road is?

(*ROBERT looks. They break away from the window.*)

ROB: So. Gary.

GARY: Yes.

ROB: Bear in mind, this session with Nick today is about mediation, it's not about revenge.

GARY: I know.

ROB: The idea is it helps the both of you.

GARY: They stole my car they could've killed me.

ROB: Nick knows that. So why did you come?

GARY: I want something. To see him. I don't know.

ROB: Gary remember, you can help this boy. Seeing you face to face, I'm hoping he'll get it, see the effects of what he does to people like you. You've both agreed to meet, and the idea with you two meeting, I don't know…maybe there's a chance he might end up being a better person for it. It's not like it's some big brainwashing thing, or like suddenly he's turned over this new leaf…but I don't know, maybe there's a chance something like this could help Nick put his record behind him. (*Beat.*) I just want you to understand, he's trying to change his own luck, okay? He's a bright lad. (*Pause.*) I'll be here at all times.

GARY: Doing what?

ROB: Nothing. Watching. I'll put in when I'm needed.

(*Beat.*) I'll go and get him.

(*ROBERT leaves the room. GARY waits, adjusts his tie, watches the fire outside. The door opens. NICK and ROBERT stand in the doorway. It is apparent from the moment we see him that NICK is in some discomfort from the heat of the room. Silence.*)

Gary. This is Nick. Shall we have a drink? Nick.

NICK: What?

(*ROBERT nods towards the tea making area.*)

(*To GARY.*) Tea? Do you take sugar?

(*NICK is pouring from the pot, GARY watches him. The cup NICK holds is shaking and the tea is missing its target.*)

ROB: Nick, why don't you put the cup down for a second, it doesn't matter.

NICK: It's okay.

ROB: The tea's going / everywhere.

GARY: Just put it down.

NICK: What?

ROB: Let him / pour another one.

GARY: Will you put it down?

(*ROBERT goes to NICK and takes the cup and coffee pot.*)

ROB: Gary, sit down.

(*He does so, slowly, choosing his chair, watching NICK.*)

ROB: Alright?

GARY: I'm holding onto the bloody chair.

NICK: (*To ROBERT.*) Fucking roasting in here, yeah?

(*Silence. ROBERT signals to NICK, regarding the biscuits.*)

NICK: (*To GARY.*) Biscuit?

GARY: Biscuit!

NICK: I was / just trying to...

ROB: Nick bought the tea / and biscuits.

GARY: What fucking Garibaldis...!!!!!!!! Jesus did you know I've got three children three children and you could've killed me?!!

ROB: Nick?

GARY: Did you?

ROB: Can you sit down Gary?

GARY: That car was my fucking car it was my property and you tried to take it I was nearly I was I was if I could get you now I'd pour that hot fucking tea all over you you're a dangerous little you're evil...

NICK: No way man.

GARY: I'm not your pals in the street.

NICK: What?

GARY: Don't use your street lingo with me 'Man'. My name's Gary.

ROB: Just call each other by your normal names, that seems the sensible thing to do.

NICK: Why's he so aggressive like this?

GARY: Me?!

ROB: Do you think this is the best way to start?

GARY: (*Heading for the door.*) It was a bad idea to begin with.

ROB: Hold on.

(*GARY stops at the door.*)

Calm down.

GARY: How do I even know he's for real?

ROB: Listen to him.

GARY: The boy stole my car.

NICK: No, I got forced into it. Some guys, they were smoking. I was stoned, we'd been hanging round all day. I'm on the dole, yeah?

GARY: But you still smoke marijuana? What other drugs do you take?

NICK: How old are you man?

GARY: Don't call me *man*.

NICK: I'm not a junkie.

GARY: No?

NICK: What you saying, you saying you never got up to nothing?

GARY: Son, you're the one with the saying to do. I can walk out of here and you're the one still needs to go to court. The pressure's all yours.

(*GARY is back at the door.*)

ROB: But you're not going to walk out are you?

GARY: What?

ROB: Not right away.

(*Silence. NICK and ROBERT are watching him. NICK uses his inhaler.*)

GARY: No.

(*GARY sits. Silence.*)

ROB: Right, let's try and start again.

Scene 14

Music plays. MARK runs onto the stage. He holds a blade to his wrist, trying to do it, to kill himself. He can't, he stops. Music ends.

Scene 15

The mediation room. Silence.

GARY: How old are you?

NICK: Nineteen.

GARY: Can't you think of anything better to do?

NICK: Like?

GARY: I don't know, you're not stupid, there must be things you can do.

NICK: I do all my letters for the dole and that yeah…? I've been for interviews, then they see where I'm living, ask about criminal records and stuff.

GARY: You're wasting your life.

NICK: You think so?

GARY: How old are you again?

NICK: Nineteen, I just told you.

GARY: (*To ROBERT.*) I was wondering…

ROB: What?

GARY: I was just wondering whether he'd go to a prison or…

NICK: No, I won't go to a prison. Young Offenders…

GARY: Institute, yes I know. (*To ROBERT.*) Isn't it Hindley for this area?

ROB: Yeah.

GARY: Kids like you hang themselves in there.

NICK: *For fuck's sake Rob!*

ROB: Was that necessary?

GARY: No, sorry, I didn't mean it like that, but I'm I'm
sitting here feeling like this is the worst day of my life
the last time I saw him he's in my car I want to kill him
and now he's here and he's he looks angelic doesn't he
he's pouring tea like he's shitting himself.

NICK: (*To ROBERT.*) You got me in here just so's he can
start insulting me, yeah?

ROB: Be serious.

NICK: You telling me to be serious! I'm here aren't I?

ROB: Yeah. Alright.

NICK: You mean, alright, shut up, only talk when I want
you to talk.

ROB: No.

(*NICK and ROBERT stare each other out. GARY watches.
Until.*)

Sorry Gary.

(*NICK stubs out his cigarette and then sucks again on his
inhaler.*)

GARY: What are you doing smoking?

NICK: Got me there man.

(*Silence.*)

GARY: So, according to you, these mates of yours forced
you into everything?

NICK: Yeah.

GARY: You could've said no.

NICK: It's the buzz...

GARY: Don't talk rubbish.

NICK: Do you want to listen or not?

ROB: Nick, can you stay sitting?

NICK: Why man...? I'm trying to make him see. I was...
I don't know, there's something goes through you...

ROB: Adrenaline.

NICK: I know what it is, yeah? I was chocka...to here... I
was shaking, and I could feel the car... Shit, when you're
off and that, you look for the pigs. Get ahead of them,

wait for the blue light in the mirror, you're taking them on.

GARY: People die from things like that.

NICK: I've never killed no one.

GARY: One day you will, if it's not you then it'll be someone else.

NICK: No.

GARY: Yes.

NICK: I'm not like that, that's why I'm here now.

GARY: You think so?

NICK: I know so.

(*Seen only by NICK, JASON enters the room.*)

JASON: Priiiiiiime tiiiiiiiiiiiiiiiiiiiiiiiime!

NICK: What the fuck...

JASON: 'I'm not like that, that's why I'm here now.' Is that your final answer?

NICK: I haven't said nothing about the shooting.

JASON: Copy.

NICK: But they're both pushing me man, it's hot, I'm feeling faint and stuff yeah?

JASON: Nick's sick and this guy's sly; it's touch and go.

NICK: I wouldn't name names.

JASON: Whatever.

(*JASON walks round the table, standing behind GARY.*)

JASON: His car yeah?

NICK: Yeah.

JASON: (*Standing behind ROBERT.*) Who's this?

NICK: Youth Justice worker.

(*He gets onto the table and stands above the two of them.*)

JASON: Get up.

(*NICK gets on the table, they regard the two men who sit below them.*)

NICK: Jase, I need to get on.

JASON: Prime time, Nick's the eager beaver student yeah?

NICK: No, I just want to explain it to him, he thinks I'm a killer.

JASON: He said you could be.

NICK: And I know I won't be.

JASON: Time says you will be.

NICK: No.

JASON: Don't fight it.

NICK: It's not my way.

JASON: (*Brandishing the gun.*) The life.

NICK: Down in hell...!

JASON: Hell? Where the fuck's hell when you're thumbing ten million notes...

NICK: Not me.

JASON: ...scorching the rubber, driving the dream time, prime time, mine mine. *Tell* him.

NICK: No.

JASON: *Tell* him you already know someone who's killed and one day you will too, copy, *you'll* kill, copy, say to him: 'You're right gormless dressing gown man, cos it's the climb, it's the LADDER.'

NICK: No!!!

JASON: Tell him motherfucker. Tell him!!

NICK: (*Screaming.*) Get out!!! Leave me alonnnnnnne!!!!!!!!
(*Silence. NICK opens his eyes and JASON is gone. He looks at GARY.*)
What?

GARY: I said, no one cares for someone like that.

NICK: No, listen, I was trying to explain, you've got to understand, I'm not proud of myself.

GARY: You shouldn't be.

ROB: He's not.

GARY: I heard him. There's something else.
(*Beat.*)
My car.

NICK: Your car?

GARY: Yes. I want to know what you did with it.

NICK: Golf.

GARY: You know what it was.

NICK: Red?

GARY: Is he taking the piss?

ROB: Nick.

GARY: Will you tell him to take this seriously?

ROB: Nick, tell Gary what happened to his car.

(*Pause.*)
NICK: Can I have one of your fags?
(*Music plays.*)

Scene 16

Seven days ago. The car.

MARK jumps out and runs round to the back of the car, throwing up. TIM waits until he's finished.

TIM: Can we get going?
MARK: I'm sick.
TIM: I know.
MARK: Fuck.
TIM: Come on.
MARK: Feel too sick.
TIM: You're nervous.
MARK: What about you?
TIM: Shitting it.
MARK: We should go back, I wanna go back.
TIM: Get in the car.
  (*TIM gets back in.*)
MARK: It's wrong, I'm telling you, everyone knows it's
  wrong...
TIM: Get in.
  (*Silence.*)
  Get in.
  (*MARK is waning.*)
  Get in.
  (*MARK gets in.*)
  We're going to need more petrol. Shall we get a tenner
  or a fiver?
MARK: What?
TIM: How much do you think we'll need?
MARK: Dunno.
TIM: Tenner might be too much, might not use it all.
  There's a garage over there.
MARK: Can you get some fags?

TIM: Could do. (*Pause.*) Ten? Twenty?
(*Music plays.*)

Scene 17

The present. Twenty-two days previously.

GARY pushes his cigarettes across the table to NICK.

NICK: Silk Cut. Nice one, better for the asthma.
GARY: Unbeatable logic.
NICK: You gonna let your kids smoke?
GARY: No.
NICK: You smoke.
GARY: Not around them. In the garden, in the pub. Not in the house.
NICK: How many a day?
GARY: Fifteen, twenty.
NICK: Cool. Look...Gary...Gazza.
GARY: Gary was fine.
NICK: Gazza's more pally.
GARY: But I'm not your pal.
NICK: Yeah. Anyway, look....
(*He looks at ROBERT. ROBERT nods him on.*)
...What I was wanting to say, the reason we're here and stuff...?
GARY: Go on.
NICK: I just wanted to see you today and apologise for what we all done to your car. It's put you through a lot of hassle, you've probably been really upset, you've got to take a day off work to come here and all that, and I understand what a fuck up it's all been. So, like...(*He shrugs. Ends. Pause. To ROBERT.*) I said it.
GARY: (*To ROBERT.*) I'm being treated like an idiot.
NICK: What?
ROB: Gary.
GARY: (*To ROBERT.*) Did you listen to that?
ROB: Of course I did.
GARY: And?

65

NICK: I was just / trying to...

ROB: (*To GARY.*) You asked him what happened to your car.

GARY: Yes, and he's changed the subject, or didn't you notice?

ROB: He was coming to something.

GARY: (*To NICK.*) Do you think you can sweet talk your way out everything?

NICK: No.

GARY: Don't start acting like you're sincere, it doesn't suit you.

NICK: Jesus, Rob, fuck this, yeah? (*To GARY.*) How come I'm so bad when you just sit there sneering all the time?

ROB: Sit down Nick.

NICK: (*To GARY.*) You're all shirt and collar, but that don't make you any better.

(*GARY stands and leans over the table.*)

GARY: I know what's right and what's wrong.

(*NICK's mobile phone rings. It breaks the moment. He doesn't answer it, until...*)

ROB: Let's take five minutes.

(*ROBERT and GARY sit, and NICK retreats to a corner of the room to take his call.*)

NICK: Yeah...?

JASON: Nicko...

(*JASON is seen only to us, crouched in his hideaway location.*)

NICK: What?.../ where are you?

JASON: Where do you think...?!! Fucking hiding, yeah?!

NICK: What you ringing me for...?

JASON: Listen, I just, I just need, I just, I just need.../

NICK: I can't speak Jase...

JASON: Please, listen...

NICK: What?

JASON: I just, I just need, I just, I just need, I just, I just need, I just, I just need, I just, I just need, I just, I just need to talk to Bootle...can you go and see him for me ...please, will you? Ask him why doesn't he answer his mobile. Copy? I just, I just need, I just, I just need to have a word with him, find out how long this sunnyshiney hideaway jobby has to go on for. It's been a week. A week!!!!! I'm desperate, I'm needing some company, yeah? I look out my window and all I can see is sand; builder's sand, dumper trucks farting, plasterers squelching. All they do round here is build! I just, I just want, I just, I just want, I just, I just want to speak to Bootle and get his opinion. Does he think the police will stop asking questions soon? Okay? okay? You go round and mention me to him yeah? Copy? Prime time. You go round and get him out the bath and ask Bootle if he wouldn't mind giving his number one assassin some sort of…

NICK: Listen Jase…

JASON: …some sort of…*Listen!!!!* I want some sort of fucking progress report!!! The days are bleeding to death, and old chimpboy here's swinging from the roofbeams, scratching his armpits. Oo-oohing oo-oohing when I see a fucking tiger go by. Oo-oohing oo-oohing like some stupid fucking tree animal no one ever stops to talk to. They're all off down to the water to get washed and kill some hippo for breakfast, and I'm doing nothing. Can you hear me? Some days I can only manage chimpspeak. YES, chimpspeak, it's not nice. Look, please, I've still got to live, you should tell Bootle that, he didn't have the right to take the bones out of my fucking body when I said I'd do his dirty business for him. I'm not some fucking sacrifice you know!!!

NICK: Listen…Jase…l can't help you alright…?

JASON: What?! You've got to…I just, I just need, I just, I just need…

NICK: I don't want nothing to do with you, / I'm doing my own stuff, don't ring me man.

JASON: Nicko… ! !

(*NICK hangs up. The lights fade on JASON's hideaway. NICK draws on his inhaler, it has run out, he shakes it, tries to get it to work. Frustrated, slightly panicked by this, he loosens his shirt, breathes for clear air, tries the inhaler again. ROBERT is at the window, looking at the fire.*)

ROB: (*To NICK.*) Who called?

(*NICK joins ROBERT at the window.*)

NICK: Cathy...what's going on...?

ROB: Fire.

GARY: Who's that then?

ROB: Social worker. And?

NICK: Told her I was busy.

GARY: Thought so.

NICK: What?

GARY: That you'd have a social worker.

NICK: Been in and out of care all my life. Old man in jail, old lady on the drink, no big deal.

GARY: I'd say it's a very big deal.

NICK: Yeah? How come you know so much?

(*NICK's breathing is getting tighter and tighter.*)

GARY: I get out, I learn things.

ROB: Gary's got his own IT business.

GARY: Designer. I design systems.

ROB: His car's important to him.

NICK: What do you design?

GARY: All sorts.

NICK: Can't learn nothing looking at a computer.

GARY: You'd be surprised. I started when I was 20.

NICK: Nice one.

GARY: Got my own house, the kids get educated, got a nice wife. It's been hard work.

NICK: How long you been married?

GARY: Twelve years.

NICK: Would you ever leave your kids?

GARY: Never.

NICK: What'd you do if one of them stole a car?

GARY: They wouldn't.

NICK: How do you know?

GARY: My kids won't do that sort of thing.

NICK: Why won't they?

GARY: I thought you were explaining yourself to me.

NICK: Do you hit them?

GARY: Never.

NICK: You shouldn't.

GARY: I don't.

NICK: What would you do if one of your kids killed
themselves?

GARY: Jesus.

NICK: Suicide's terrible, yeah?

GARY: (*To ROBERT.*) Aren't we going off on a tangent here?

NICK: No, listen, it's just...

(*TIM and MARK move from the car, and stand looking out
over the edge of the cliff. As NICK continues, they take in the
wind and the sound of the sea.*)

NICK: I mean...there's these two guys...my age more or
less, two of them...they had this car... I...well...it was
your car...

GARY: My car?

NICK: Four guys stole your wheels.

GARY: I know.

NICK: So that's me, another kid, and then these two guys
I'm telling you about... Last week, they're in your car
and they went to the coast. They drove it off a cliff.

GARY: They did what?

NICK: I saw them a few nights before, I didn't know what
they were planning.

GARY: Is that what / they did?!

NICK: They've got this Mini-DV thing, and I'm just...But
like, you were wanting to know what happened to your
car. I didn't know how to tell you.

GARY: They drove it off a cliff!!?

NICK: Why'd they have / to kill themselves...?

GARY: But...but...

NICK: It's in my head.

GARY: They....??

NICK: I got this note from Mark.../...Makes me sick we
ever nicked it.

GARY: I don't believe you just told me that, they drove it
off a fucking cliff!!!

ROB: Cars do get written off Gary, you must've half
expected it.

GARY: What??? But why…why did they just… I… (*He is slower, realising. He stops. Silence*) They killed themselves? (*Long silence.*)
Jesus.
(*NICK is breathing heavy, dragging on his inhaler, still panicked that he can't get anything from it. ROBERT goes to him.*)
ROB: You okay Nick?
NICK: My inhaler's fucked.
(*The lights change. The sound of the sea grows.*)

Scene 18

Seven days previously. A cliff edge.

TIM swigs from a can of beer, drinking it all the way down in one long gulp. MARK shivers.

MARK: S'gone cold…
TIM: Wind's picking up.
(*Silence.*)
MARK: Can you swim?
TIM: Like a fish.
MARK: I cheated to get my swimming badge. I was ten. We had to swim from one end of the pool to the other ennit, the night we did it, the pool was mega, kids everywhere. We all had to set off together ennit. Half way up the baths some kid started to panic, the lifeguards jumped in to rescue him. It was dead busy, people screaming, shouting, the kid drowning. No one saw me and I stopped at the side ennit, got my breath. Some instructor said we ought to carry on, the boy was safe. Rest of us got to the end, yeah? Fucking swimming instructor says gather round; she knows some of us had to stop ennit, but some of us didn't, some of us got to the end. So being honest, which of you completed the length without stopping? Hands start going up ennit.
TIM: What about yours?
MARK: Dead slowly, like I wasn't really lying.
(*Pause.*)

See those waves out there, no one survives waves like
that. Once we're over the edge, we'll be swallowed up.

TIM: Jonah and the whale.

MARK: I'll swim for it.

TIM: Get fucked.

MARK: I'll swim for it, I know I will, I'll have to try.

(*TIM is laughing.*)

What?... What?

(*TIM puts the Mini-DV on the ground.*)

What you doing?

TIM: Leaving it. Get in.

(*No answer.*)

Get in.

MARK: Why?

TIM: *Get in.*

MARK: Why...

TIM: Get in...

MARK: ...why do you want me to die, / it's you...

TIM: Because there's nothing for you.

MARK: But I want there to be. That's just you telling me.
How do you know?

TIM: If I die, yeah? and you don't, you'll go down more,
you'll do things you can't live with. I'm doing it for you,
for both of us.

MARK: No, you're doing it cos you're weak, cos you're
tired and you're scared of what you can't get...

TIM: (*Exploding.*) I'm doing it cos you fucked up my life...

MARK: Not me, ennit.

TIM: Yeah, you. IT'S YOU AND IT'S ALL THE OTHER
FUCKERS. I'D TAKE AS MANY OF YOU WITH ME
AS I COULD...I'D FUCKING...I'D FUCKING.........

MARK: We could get help ennit.

TIM: You mean doctors, pills, cos we're depressed.

MARK: I dunno...I...

TIM: You ever been in a junk yard?

MARK: What...?

TIM: ...somewhere where they crush cars like this
one...machines, the noise, the grinding...like someone's

draining blood out of you…So much grinding…
machines grinding things…grinding things so they don't
look like they ever did…
(*Silence*)

TIM: Do what you want. Do what the fuck you want.

(*TIM goes back to the car. Waits. MARK looks at the Mini-
DV, out at the sea. Finally, he goes back to the car and gets
in.*
Music plays.)

Scene 19

The present. Twenty-two days previously.
*NICK is sucking on his inhaler. GARY broods for his car, his
head in his hands. Silence whilst NICK gets his breath.
Until…*

ROB: You alright Nick?

NICK: It's too hot in here man, can't we go outside or
something?

ROB: In a minute.

NICK: I need some space, got you two pressing me all the
time. (*To GARY.*) You wanted to know about your car, I
told you, yeah?

ROB: No one's pressing you.

NICK: Rob, I'm really struggling man, my chest and stuff.

ROB: The quicker we move on, the quicker we can finish.

NICK: Yeah, outside.

(*ROB is silent.*)

You're ruled by the fucking book. Can't go outside, have
to stay in here, why?

ROB: Because you don't always get what you want, that's
the way it is Nick. Alright?

NICK: Should never've bothered with this man.

ROB: You need to see it through. I asked Gary to come, I
don't want to let him down. I don't want to let you down.

NICK: How? He's alright, it's his car got nicked, he's not
the one in the shit.

ROB: You asked me to help you.

NICK: Yeah, but it's like you're watching everything I say, I can't talk to him honest and stuff cos I can see you there.

ROB: I have to be here.

NICK: Yeah, but it's like, I need to ask things.

ROB: No one's stopping you asking Gary questions.

NICK: I wanted to ask him about his job...whether he thinks I could do something like that, get myself sorted. But I don't feel natural, seeing you there, it's like you're my dad or something, telling me what to do all the time.

ROB: Nick, you've already proved what happens if you don't have someone 'telling' you what to do. You end up in situations like this.

NICK: Yeah.

ROB: So it's my job to supervise you.

NICK: Don't want no fucking supervising.

ROB: Well then you're going to end up in the shit all your life aren't you? Hanging onto people, like a parasite, sucking the energy out of people. I've had it...you know? I've tried what I can with you mate... I...

NICK: And like you can really look into the future, yeah? You don't know nothing about me.

(*Stand off. Pause.*)

ROB: Sorry, I didn't mean to judge you like that. It's just...

GARY: (*To NICK.*) He wants to save you.

ROB: What?

GARY: (*To ROBERT.*) And the boy won't let you. He's got you so you don't know which way to turn. People need boundaries, you don't let him know how far he can go.

ROB: Yes I do.

GARY: No you don't, you're excusing him all the time, you take his side: 'He's trying to change his own luck. He's a bright lad'. And just now, you get frustrated with him, and then you apologise, like you might've hurt his feelings or something.

ROB: Gary, when you're in my position, then maybe you'll understand how to go about things.

GARY: Perhaps, but I'm just listening to the way he talks to you, how do you put up with that? So far I've spent my whole time here being offered biscuits, going round in circles while he gives me smart arse answers, listening to his point of view.../

ROB: We've / been trying to consider both sides...

GARY: ...where he's been brought up, his drug habit, his 'nasty' friends who make him do things against his will, and I listen, and I wait, and it's like...you don't do anything...

ROB: What is it / you'd like me to do?

GARY: Focus the conversation completely on me. About how I was wronged, get him to talk about what he thinks I've been through, not just having to miss a day at work, but what it's done to me. Crime is about the victim not the criminal.

NICK: I'm not a criminal.

GARY: No?

(*Now NICK is really struggling for breath, finding it hard to speak.*)

NICK: What's the crack with you man? What you frightened of?

ROB: Nick...

GARY: I'm an ordinary bloke, thousands of people like me, I'm *ordinary*. I don't want....and I'm *frightened* of people like YOU, I get frightened when I see you on street corners and in subways, that's what I'm frightened of.

ROB: This isn't what you came here for Gary.

GARY: Yes it fucking is.

ROB: No, / you didn't, you...

GARY: Do you think I'd come here for any other reason than to look this little bastard in the eye and tell him what I think of him. (*To NICK*) I don't want to know how 'hard' it's been for you, I don't care about your fucking upbringing, your fucking... (*To ROB.*) This is actually great, this forum idea of yours Robert.../

ROB: *It's not a / forum*

GARY: ...yeah, you should do it more often...

ROB: Alright, / you've made your point, you've had your fun...

GARY: ...bring it on! The whole country can sign up, right? Face our fucking enemies.

ROB: Listen to yourself...

GARY: ...remind ourselves what the world's really like.../

ROB: What you're doing is unacceptable.

NICK: You're a stuck up bastard.

GARY: (*To ROBERT.*) See! So now either ask him to apologise, or tell him he's lost his chance and the session's over.

NICK: You only came here to make me look like a twat, right?

GARY: No, I came here because I want you to start learning some lessons.

ROB: He is, give him the chance, he will. (*To NICK.*) You okay?

NICK: I need to get outside for a bit.

GARY: The chance?

NICK: Rob...

GARY: Robert, I work hard...

ROB: No one's disputing that.

NICK: Rob.

ROB: (*To NICK.*) Try not to get so / uptight.

NICK: My chest's / killing me.

GARY: I build the country, I do my bit.

ROB: We all do that.

NICK: Rob.

GARY: So you'll understand my point.

NICK: Robert?

ROB: It's the sort of.../ point I hear all the time.

NICK: Rob.

GARY: Good. Because if I don't make any cash...

NICK: Fuck.

GARY: ...then I don't keep the house.

NICK: Fuck.

ROB: We know all this.

NICK: Rob come / on man.

GARY: I don't keep the car.

NICK: I need some fresh / air.

GARY: So who's making it easy?

ROB: Let me sort / Nick out.

GARY: For me.

NICK: Rob?

GARY: People like me.

NICK: Rob.

GARY: Where do we stand?

NICK: Rob!

ROB: Certainly / not together.

GARY: People / like me.

NICK: This is doing / my fucking head in.

ROB: (*To GARY.*) You want an easy life…?

NICK: Fuck this. / Just…

ROB: In a second Nick.

GARY: Who's giving / people like me a chance?

NICK: Fuck / it!

ROB: We all / want an easy life.

NICK: Fuck it!!!!!!

(*GARY and ROBERT stop.*)

NICK: (*To GARY.*) Fuck people like you!

(*Beat. Then GARY pushes the chairs aside and lunges for
NICK. They struggle and ROBERT fights to pull them apart.
Suddenly NICK stops, hyperventilating.*)

GARY: What's happening!?

ROB: He's having an asthma attack.

GARY: Do something…

(*From here, the focus swaps backwards and forwards from
ROB's apartment, to the car and to JASON's hideaway
location. NICK is on his knees, gasping. In the car, TIM
speaks to MARK.*)

TIM: We'll get over the edge easy enough.

MARK: Yeah.

TIM: Shame to bust it up, nice wheels.

(*Pause.*)

MARK: Just fucking do it.

(*TIM starts the car. The engine revs, and NICK drops to the
floor.*)

GARY: What are you doing?…what is it.?.!!

MARK: No, no, no, no, no, no, no, no, no, no, no, no, no,
no, no, no, no, no, NO!!!

(*NICK tries to speak to him, but has no breath. They stare
into each other's eyes. GARY waits at NICK's side as the boy*

loses consciousness, and ROBERT starts to give him mouth to mouth. On the cliff, the speed of the car increases and builds to a crescendo of sound.)

GARY: No, no, no...

(At the same time, JASON appears, dials on his mobile, growing more frantic as he fails to get through to whoever he is calling. In the car, the boys fall forward as they go over the cliff. The sound of the engine is deafening and then cuts out.

Blackout. The lights come back up, there is just the sound of the wind blowing, and the waves moving. GARY is at NICK's side and ROBERT, less and less, tries to bring NICK back. It is a futile series of actions until he stops, and he and GARY kneel at the dead boy's side.)

Scene 20

The present. JASON's hideaway location.

JASON, still with his mobile, talks quietly.

JASON: I miss you... Why didn't we speak for so long? I can't remember much at the moment, my head's gone all grey lines, I'm the TV they couldn't tune, the kid you couldn't tame. Dad, it's prime time talking to you, I'd love to be there with you... I'm not that far away as it goes... Dad, do you know about being alone? Copy. See me? See inside my head? See those feelings over there, see them? They're whispering: 'Jase, Jase, Jase is a case.' I shut the stable door before you were ever a horse and there was ever a stable or ever a door. I'm ahead of the pack, and bottom of the heap... Dad, did the San Andreas fault ever fall in like you said it would? What about the Marie Celeste? Did anyone ever come back for their dinner? You're good at stories, that's something I really miss... No, I can't, I can't see you, can't see anyone, not till the police stop asking questions...

(He hangs up. Music plays.)

Scene 21

The present. The mediation room.

The fire outside has increased and a red hue can be seen through the window. GARY watches it.

GARY: Have you seen out there? That fire's moving closer.
   (*Silence.*)
ROB: (*Quietly.*) We ought to shoot off.
GARY: Right.
   (*Pause*)
   Has the ambulance gone? Are you going to the hospital?
ROB: I need to call some people, but yes, I'm....
   (*He stops.*)
GARY: Okay. Well.
   (*Silence.*)
   He was carrying this.
ROB: Sorry?
GARY: Your nice young man, he was carrying this.
   (*GARY goes to ROBERT and holds a metal 'knife' up before him.*)
ROB: Nick?
GARY: It's some sort of home made knife, time spent
   deliberately filing it to a point. Nasty.
ROB: I can see what it is.
GARY: It was in his pocket.
ROB: Put it down.
GARY: I can't get this thought out of my head see if he was
   so intent so determined on getting on the straight and
   narrow just like you said he was then what was he doing
   carrying one of these?
ROB: I don't know.
GARY: Give him the chance you said.
ROB: Gary, you can't prove he intended using it on you for
   Christ's sake.
GARY: No but what about on somebody else what about on
   another day? (*Pause.*) So what do I think?
ROB: Think what you like.

GARY: Tell me, you're the mediator.

ROB: You think how close you came to him, you think how today was our chance as much as Nick's.

GARY: You'd go down with the ship wouldn't you?

ROB: Probably.

GARY: I'll tell you what I think. He was a nuisance to the public.

ROB: I need to contact Nick's parents.

GARY: He attacked me.

ROB: You went for him.

GARY: Under provocation.

ROB: You're a bloody fool.

(*GARY turns the knife suddenly and grabs ROBERT, holding the blade against his bare flesh.*)

GARY: Have you ever been burgled?

ROB: What?

GARY: Have you ever been mugged?

ROB: No.

GARY: So how do you know what it feels like...?! I'll cut you, hold still...

ROB: Gary!

GARY: I said hold still...

(*GARY pushes ROBERT free.*)

ROB: You're a fucking maniac.

GARY: Now you'll want to take a run at me. You will, even you.

(*Long long silence.*)

ROB: Sometimes you fool yourself, you believe you can make a difference...

GARY: Not in his case.

ROB: First time I met Nick, Michelle brought him here. (*He looks at GARY.*) My daughter. He stood there at the window and named all the cars he could see on the ring road. Trouble. I could see it the minute he walked in; what the fuck was she doing with a kid like him? But a big smile, big energy, you couldn't help liking him. Maybe that's what I was hoping you'd see.

GARY: I saw a car thief, a foul mouth good for nothing who didn't know the meaning of a smile.

ROB: You were crying when he was lying on the floor...

(*Beat.*)

GARY: What?

ROB: Why did you come here today? To measure yourself, put your life next to Nick's, reassure yourself how you're a good citizen.

GARY: I am a good citizen.

ROB: Of course you are, you don't break the law, you're married...

GARY: What is this?

ROB: I'm just, I'm asking...you...me...it's a question. .Who do you care for?

GARY: Family, friends.

ROB: Beyond that...

GARY: What?

ROB: After family and friends...who else...?

GARY: Robert, you're making this personal. (*He indicates the room, the day they've had.*) All 'this' isn't my fault.

ROB: No, and I suppose you've got your own life to live.

GARY: Yeah, and why not? (*Beat.*) Why the fuck shouldn't I?

(*They face each other. Until...*)

GARY: I suppose these other 'forums' you've done / weren't quite so...

ROB: *They're not forums.*

GARY: Well what then? (*Beat.*) What exactly is it that you're doing Robert?

ROB: (*Evenly.*) It's what I do. I don't need to explain myself.

GARY: I just don't know how you can care so much. Day in, day out, these people walking through your door.

(*Silence, until...*)

GARY: I'm going to the hospital. Do you need a lift?

ROB: (*Shaking his head.*) I'll follow you.

(*GARY leaves. ROBERT stares out at the fire. Music plays and JASON appears, followed by the other boys who wait behind him, he has the gun. He speaks to ROBERT.*)

JASON: There's a saying goes like this: make a car, sell a
car, buy a car, drive a car, but never, ever, *love* a car. In a
darkened room, Tim, Marky and Nick are watched by
Jason from the window of Jason's hideaway location.
He's been there weeks and still no one's come. It's
obvious that there's this story of four boys who stole a
car and paid for it with their lives. There's a saying that's
going to be used to describe them, something like: 'They
were stupid and feckless and they wasted their lives.'
(*JASON holds the gun to his temple, pulling the trigger with
each 'Click'.*)
Click... Click. The barrel goes round. I'm waiting for it,
it's going to come. Copy. Meanwhile, I'm thinking: that
guy didn't trim his hedge evenly, that car's got a stolen
number plate...stop it!! can you stop *thinking* about cars
for just one minute!... What I'm thinking, what I'm
thinking is: for some people, and the way they live, it's
got to be roulette. Russian roulette. Click... (*Long
silence.*) Click...
(*JASON closes his eyes, waiting for the bullet he's sure will
come. He pulls it, nothing. He pulls the trigger again.*)

Blackout.

RAW

Characters

LEX
eighteen

TRAINERS (TRAIN)
nineteen

ADDY
twenty-five

LORNA
eighteen

RUEBEN (RUBE)
thirty-five

SHELLEY (SHELL)
twenty-six

The present day. Winter.

Raw was first produced by Theatre Absolute, in a co-production with the Belgrade Theatre, Coventry, and Pleasance Theatre, London. *Raw* was first performed at the Belgrade Theatre on 17 July 2001. It then transferred to the 2001 Edinburgh Fringe Festival, performing at the Pleasance Cavern, where it was awarded a Scotsman Fringe First for Outstanding New Work. The cast and production team was as follows:

TRAINERS, Samantha Power

LORNA, Claire Corbett

LEX, Jo Joyner

ADDY, Paul Simpson

RUEBEN, Gary Cargill

SHELLEY, Rebecca Manley

Director, Mark Babych

Set Design, Dominie Hooper

Lighting Design, Paul Bull

Soundscape, Andy Garbi

Stage Manager, Jennie Anderson

Technician, Claire Dickinson

Producer, Julia Negus

Raw toured nationally in Spring 2002. The cast and production team was as follows:

TRAINERS, Samantha Power

LORNA, Claire Corbett

LEX, Jo Joyner

ADDY, Graeme Hawley

RUEBEN, Gary Cargill

SHELLEY, Rebecca Manley

Director, Mark Babych

Set Design, Dominie Hooper

Lighting Design, Paul Bull

Soundscape, Andy Garbi

Stage Manager, Emma Baron

Technician, Avril Mason

Producer, Julia Negus

Notes

1. In general, when Lorna speaks, she issues a swift monotone through a low mutter. For example, 'We get the number forty bus and go all the way into town, we don't get off at the usual stop,' should 'read' something like this: 'Wegetthenumberforty busandgoallthewayintotown,wedon'tgetoffattheusualstop.' Not everyone can always tell what she is saying.

2. When Trainers says '…yumlike…', it is not extended, it is quick, like a glottal shock; a preface to most things that she says. This is an example upon which an actor can build; it may be more of a sound than words.

3. The action of the play should feel continuous, no obvious scene breaks. There should be an intense use of soundscape and music which bleeds from one scene to another so that the pressure of the world in the play feels relentless and unbearable; mirroring the pressure and extremity within the characters' lives.

4. The symbol / indicates a point of interruption.

1

Tuesday. On a train. 4:45pm.

Music plays.

There is the sound of a train moving: fast, screeching across the tracks. Abrasive and uncomfortable. We can make out the shapes of LEX, TRAINERS and LORNA.

LEX watches a young BOY who is pissed. He lies across both sets of seats, his arse hanging between the two of them, a pair of headphones on his ears, a cap pulled down over his eyes. He is an amusement, singing, ridiculous in his drunkenness.

LEX is looking at the BOY, looking away, looking back again, smiling to herself. The BOY slips further between the seats so that now his fat belly is exposed and his arse is threatening to come out of his trousers. LEX is smiling at him.

Gradually, as the rhythm of the train continues and the BOY slips further between the seats and nothing seems to change, things do change. The BOY suddenly looks up, drunk. His eyes stop on LEX. Her amusement is seen to alter, and words start to form on her lips.

LEX: ...you got the wr you got on the wr you got the wr
    you got on the wr you got the wr you got on the wr...
    (*The other two girls watch as LEX continues.*)
    You got the wr you got on the wr you got the wr you got
    on the wr didn't you get I think you got you just got on
    the wr...wrong. You got the wr you got on the wr you
    got the wr you got on the wr didn't you get I think you
    got you just got on the wrong. Train. (*Now LEX walks to
    the boy, stands over him, still speaking.*) You got the wr you /
    you got on the wr...
BOY: What?
LEX: Did you get I think you / got you just got on the wr...
    Wrong.
BOY: Fuck / off.
LEX: Did you get I think you got you just got on the
    wrong. Train.

(*Music bleeds in against the sound of the train. LEX raises her fist and sends the BOY flying backwards. The music still plays, but then suddenly it seems to come out of 'the other side': through the music there is the metal echo of LEX breathing, gasping as she bends to look at the BOY, her heart beating and the fast rhythm of the words still heard, but distant, a different part of her. She pounces on him and punches him in the face, several times, until he is still.*

LEX leans over the BOY's face, pinching his cheeks, flicking his ears, dribbling a long line of spit onto his face. She gets up and walks back to TRAINERS and LORNA who watch her, both shocked by what she has done. LORNA and TRAINERS both go to the BOY, LORNA touches the back of his head, her hand is covered in blood.

Whilst the two girls are at the BOY's side, LEX sits; going into herself as the moment passes, staring at the floor in a fight to compose herself.

The music starts to fade and the rhythm and noise of the train comes back the stronger. On and on, the BOY on the floor and LORNA staring at the blood on her hand. The train noise builds and builds until it shifts and breaks.)

2

LEX's flat. 5:45pm.

LEX, LORNA, TRAINERS and ADDY. LORNA is at the Venetian blinds, opening and closing them; manic, fevered.

TRAIN: ...yumlike...
LEX: Lorna.
LORNA: What? I am, I'm / listening...
LEX: You're not.
LORNA: I am.
LEX: You're not, you're fucking not, you're staring out the window, you're doing the blinds /
LORNA: Best thing for us, / to do the blinds...
LEX: Yeah I know it is, but I'm trying to tell you.
LORNA: I know you are, and I'm trying to listen, but I'm all like...

LEX: What?

LORNA: I said, I know you are, and I'm trying to listen, but I'm all like…

LEX: *Fuck's sake.*

(*Silence.*)

LORNA: Yeah, so go on, carry on, I'm sorry, carry on.

LEX: What?

LORNA: I said, go on, carry on, I'm sorry, carry on.

LEX: You need to let me finish / what I'm trying to tell you.

LORNA: I will, but I can't at the moment because I can't stop shaking, yeah?

LEX: What?

LORNA: I SAID, I WILL, BUT I CAN'T AT THE MOMENT BECAUSE I CAN'T STOP SHAKING / YEAH?

LEX: YOU SHOUTING AT ME!?…

LORNA: NO!!!!!

(*Silence.*)

LEX: Look, no one saw us. Alright? There was no one else on the train, so no police are going to come knocking on the door. No one saw us legging it. So no one knows it was us, yeah?

ADDY: How'd you know for definite?

LEX: Because I do.

ADDY: She's scared.

LEX: Yeah, and I'm trying to explain, but she won't listen. Lorna…

LORNA: What?

LEX: You don't need to keep…

LORNA: You got a spare ciggie…?

(*LEX gets her fags out, gives one to LORNA.*)

LEX: You don't need to keep shaking cos no one…

LORNA: You got a light…

LEX: *For fuck's sake.* (*She lights LORNA's fag.*) I'm saying: you don't need to keep shaking cos no one saw us; train's empty, / station's empty…

LORNA: CCTV.

TRAIN: …yumlike…

LEX: What?

LORNA: CCTV. CCTV's everywhere.

LEX: Ads, will you tell her there wasn't any fucking CCTV on the train, tell her it's just us knows about it.

LORNA: Us? I never did anything. It wasn't me went and killed / some kid...

TRAIN: ...yumlike, we didn't kill him.

LORNA: That boy wasn't doing anything wrong, he was just sitting there, and you just went for him, like you're fucking... We're going to get caught, you go round doing things like that and we're going to get caught...

LEX: It's not the first fucking time / I trashed someone...

LORNA: Yeah, but not like that, *never* like that before.

LEX: So what you saying?

LORNA: I'm saying, I don't want anything to do with it.

LEX: Yeah? Well I'M SAYING IT'S A BIT FUCKING LATE NOW ISN'T IT!!

(*LEX pushes LORNA across the kitchen, ADDY leaps up to defend LORNA. He is followed by TRAINERS, who in the heat of the moment crashes into LEX and sends her reeling backwards onto her arse. LORNA retreats, chewing on a piece of bread that she fetches from her pocket.*)

TRAIN: ...yumlike...

(*LEX lies on the floor, momentarily stunned.*)

(*To LORNA; quieter.*) ...yumlike you seen what you're doing?

(*LEX gets up, pulls TRAINERS round. Silence. Then.*)

LEX: Do your counts.

(*No one moves.*)

Do your fucking counts.

(*Unable to resist LEX's will, the others move to their 'stations'. ADDY at the lights, TRAINERS over a floorboard, LORNA at the blinds. ADDY starts the lights, banging on the wall with an off beat; on, off, on, off, tap, tap; on, off, on, off, tap, tap. This rhythm is matched by TRAINERS who stamps on the floorboard, and then accentuated further by LORNA who opens and closes the blinds in a similar rhythm. They watch LEX, LEX watches them as they build the 'counts', the rhythm*) *growing faster and stronger. Then the doorbell rings. Sudden silence. Then.)*

ADDY: Fuck...

(They spring from their positions, tidying the room, moving chairs. TRAINERS heads for the door.)

LEX: What you doing?

TRAIN: ...yumlike...

LEX: Leave it...

(TRAINERS goes.)

Trainers...

(The others wait. More tension. TRAINERS returns with RUEBEN.)

RUBE: Alright?

LEX: Who's this?

TRAIN: Rube.

LEX: *(To TRAINERS.)* What?... You mean we're fucking... and you're just... *(To RUBE.)* You want to wait outside?

RUBE: It's raining.

TRAIN: ...yumlike I asked him to come round.

LEX: We're in the middle of stuff.

TRAIN: ...he's sound, / it's alright.

LEX: Trainers, I just told you to do something, so don't fucking ignore me, you know what I'm saying?

TRAIN: Yeah, and you just went and did what you wanted tonight, no fucking warning, nothing, and so bang we're all in the shit...yumlike, so we're square, yeah?

(Beat.)

LEX: I think you better fuck off.

TRAIN: ...what?

LEX: You heard.

TRAIN: Lex...?

LEX: People, all the time, acting like they think they can walk all over me.

TRAIN: ...yumlike no one's doing nothing, yeah?... yumlike, you're lucky with us lot...yumlike, me, I'm solid with you, me and you run the crew yeah?...and I'm fucking *solid*, one hundred per cent.

LEX: Don't get carried away Trainers.

TRAIN: Carried away? About what?…yumlike, you need
me…
(*Pause.*)

RUBE: What is all this?

ADDY: That's our business.

RUBE: Maybe you should calm down a bit.
(*He holds out a hand to LEX. She ignores it.*)
Rueben.

LEX: Meaning?

RUBE: I'm a mate of Trainers. She asked me along to meet
you all, but it all feels a bit…you know?

LEX: What?
(*Beat. He shrugs.*)

RUBE: Aggressive.
(*Pause. She stares at him.*)

LEX: I'll deal with the nutter later. Listen, yous all better
decide what you want to do. Ads?

ADDY: No problems. Sorry about earlier, yeah?

LEX: Lorna…?
(*Eyes at the floor, she nods, acquiecesing under the force of
LEX's personality, still chewing on her bread.*)

TRAIN: …yumlike…

LEX: I thought I just told you to fuck off.

TRAIN: Lex…yumlike, why you doing this to me?
(*No answer.*)
…I'm asking you.
(*Silence. TRAINERS waits still. RUBE steps towards her.
She shakes him away.*)
No…yumlike fuck it… (*To LEX.*) and fuck you as well…
(*TRAINERS goes. LORNA follows her. Music plays.
RUEBEN stays. ADDY and LEX wait, watching him,
amused. The music stops.*)

RUBE: (*To LEX.*) Do you want a ciggie?
(*No answer.*)
This your place? (*Pause.*) So you're the mastermind
behind all this graffiti mugging stuff.
(*LEX looks at him.*)
Trainers was telling me. She thinks you're a bit of a star,
dead nifty with the old hands. Some poor granny walks

by, she gets her face painted and her bag snatched. Very
neat.

LEX: How come you're still here exactly?

RUBE: Trainers invited me. She left, and I stayed.

(*Pause.*)

LEX: How d'you know her?

RUBE: She went down the youth centre I work at. I've
known her since she was fifteen, / spotty face, pigtails.

LEX: *Youth* centre?

RUBE: Yeah.

LEX: You work down a youth centre?

RUBE: Part time sessional stuff, yeah. Do a bit of drawing,
run a few art projects.

LEX: Why?

RUBE: Why not?

LEX: Do you do those cosy little day trips out to the
museum and the theatre, and stuff?

RUBE: Of course. (*Pause.*) Is that what you think it's like?

(*Beat.*)

LEX: I don't think nothing.

(*Silence.*)

Anyway, it's not nice, yeah? Forcing your way into
someone else's house. I'm only eighteen, I'm a
vulnerable young woman. (*Beat.*) I've got to go and see
someone.

RUBE: Right.

(*She stands. Shows him the door.*)

LEX: See you.

(*Music plays.*)

3

LEX's flat. 8:05pm.

*Music plays. ADDY is alone at the light switch, turning it on, turning
it off, turning it on, turning it off; at the same time as he does this,
he taps the wall on an off beat.*

LORNA enters.

LORNA: Stop now, yeah?...

(*She starts to pull his hand away.*)

ADDY: Lorna...

LORNA: ...you'll be fucking... Just stop now...

ADDY: *Lorna...*

LORNA: *Stop now...*

ADDY: Lor...

(*He pulls her hands to her side. Long silence.*)

LORNA: That boy on the train might be dead.

ADDY: He won't be...

(*She moves away.*)

...we would've heard something...

(*She goes to the table, gets out a pen and paper. Silence.*)

Are you alright?

LORNA: Write me some words.

ADDY: What?

LORNA: Write me some words.

ADDY: In a minute. Do the blinds first, you need to do your counts.

LORNA: No. You can write your name down the bookies, so you can write me some words, yeah?

ADDY: What?

LORNA: I said, you can write your name down the bookies, so you can write me some words. Here, pen, paper. Write it, while she's out, the sort of things I need to say...

ADDY: Like what?

LORNA: I don't know what, that's why I want you to help me.

ADDY: Well how the fuck should I know? I don't know what you want to say...

LORNA: I want to say that I want to go... That I'm...

(*Long long silence.*)

ADDY: If you try and leg it, you're going to make problems.

LORNA: She won't know where I've gone.

ADDY: She'll find out.

LORNA: You really think she's going to be that bothered?

ADDY: I just know what she's like.

LORNA: Why'd you defend her? *What's so important we're fucking everything up...?*
(*No answer. Silence.*)
You didn't see what she did on that train.
ADDY: What?
LORNA: I said, you didn't see / what she did on that train.
ADDY: I know.
LORNA: You should want to help me.
ADDY: I do. (*Pause.*) Just try and start again.
LORNA: Addy, please.
ADDY: She knows what the crack is. I'll talk to her, I'll try and get her to calm things down a bit. Yeah?
(*ADDY and LORNA stare at each other. The paper and the pen still between them.*
Music plays.)

4

TRAINERS' flat, 7:15pm, and SHELLEY's house, 8:05pm.

LEX drags TRAINERS from a chair, twisting her arm behind her back and pushing her face against the wall

TRAIN: ...yumlike I'm sorry!!! / I just wanted you to meet Rube...
LEX: Just say it and / I'll let you go...
TRAIN: ...yumlike I thought / you'd be pleased. I just wanted to show him what we've been doing...
LEX: Are you stupid, or what? Say it.
TRAIN: ...yumlike...
LEX: 'I'm trying to.../take things over.'
TRAIN: ...yumlike...
LEX: 'But I can't, because I can't handle things the way Lex does,' yeah?
(*TRAINERS bites LEX's hand. LEX screams in pain and she lashes out, sending TRAINERS backwards across the room. LEX starts to speak, whispered at first, until the words become clearer. As she speaks, so does TRAINERS.*)

LEX: Ra the mess... I could ra, ra your face. Ra the mess...
I could ra, ra your face... Ra... Ra the mess... I could ra,
ra your face. Ra the mess...I could ra, ra your face...
Ra... Ra the mess... I could ra, ra your face. Ra the
mess... I could ra, ra your face... Ra...

TRAIN: ...yumlike... I'm sorry alright?... What you
doing?... Look, I just asked Rube over cos I was telling
him about you, yumlike, how brilliant you are...it
doesn't matter what you did on that train...yumlike, I
never said nothing against it... I wouldn't do stuff to
upset you... What you saying...? Lex...?

LEX: Ra the mess... I could ra, ra your face. Ra the mess...
I could ra, ra your face... Ra. Ra the mess... I could ra,
ra your face. Ra the mess... I could ra, ra your face. Ra.
Ra the mess... I could ra, ra your face. Ra the mess... I
could ra, ra your face... Ra.

(*LEX grabs TRAINERS in a headlock and starts punching
her in the face.*)

Don't bite my fucking hand. Don't bring people into my
house who aren't invited. Don't tell people what we do.
Don't try and act like you can be leader. *And don't make
me look like a fucking idiot in front of everyone else!!*

(*TRAINERS drops like a brick to the floor. She is out cold.*)

SHELL: Sarnie?

LEX: No thanks.

SHELL: Bread and jam?

LEX: Still no.

SHELL: Apple?

LEX: I don't want nothing, yeah?

SHELL: Coke?

(*Beat.*)

LEX: Go on.

(*SHELLEY pours a glass of Coke and LEX crosses from
TRAINERS' to SHELLEY's place.*)

SHELL: So what do we owe the honour? You hear we won
the lottery, or something?

LEX: ?

SHELL: Sense of humour.

(*SHELLEY sees LEX's bitten finger.*)

What you been doing?

LEX: Visiting.

(*LEX downs her Coke. Gasps.*)

SHELL: Who were you fighting with?

LEX: Trainers.

SHELL: I thought you were mates.

(*No answer. SHELLEY starts cleaning LEX's cut.*)

You can't just come running / when it suits, yeah?

LEX: I didn't. (*Beat.*) I was passing.

(*Silence.*)

What you been up to?

SHELL: This and that... Jacking in the fags.

LEX: You're always jacking in the fags.

SHELL: Three weeks.

(*Silence.*)

LEX: Your Carl not around?

SHELL: Not at the moment.

LEX: You mean he's back on remand?

SHELL: Sorry, was that a joke?

LEX: Dunno.

(*SHELLEY eyeballs her.*)

Shell, it was a laugh, yeah?

(*SHELLEY puts the TCP away.*)

Listen, some people are into the old family tree stuff, right? Nephews, nieces, brother-in-laws. I just think it's a bit, it's just not me, yeah? You want me to think like you, and I don't want to think like you. I want to think like me.

SHELL: Exactly. And where does that get you?

(*No answer.*)

Anyway, you just be what you want to be, you know what I'm saying?

LEX: You don't mean that.

SHELL: Yes I do.

LEX: No you don't, I know you don't.

SHELL: Don't be such a smart arse, yeah?

(*SHELLEY puts a large plaster over the cut.*)

How long since I seen you?

LEX: Forget.

SHELL: And now you are here, what we doing?

LEX: You started it.

SHELL: I know. (*Pause.*) So you been keeping alright?

LEX: Not so bad.

SHELL: You hungry?

LEX: Bit.

SHELL: I've got some leftovers; sausages, peas, potatoes…

(*TRAINERS coughs, choking on some blood. The sound breaks the moment between LEX and SHELLEY. It takes LEX back to the memory of what she has just done.*
During this next section, SHELLEY checks her cigarettes, counting the fags left in the packet.)

LEX: Trainers…?

(*LEX stares at TRAINERS, who still groans and struggles for breath, only half conscious. LEX is both terrified and exhilarated by the mess she has made of her mate's face.*
TRAINERS begins to shake, like a fit is passing over her. LEX notices; panic fills her as TRAINERS' behaviour becomes more and more extreme. She puts a hand to her forehead.)
Why you so hot…?

(*The fit continues. LEX pulls at TRAINERS, as a new convulsion hits her. Instinctively, LEX grabs TRAINERS' hand, whispering.*)

…fuck…good come good come good come…fuck's sake…good come good come…good come good come good come…

(*The fit continues as the words that LEX speaks, barely decipherable, but totally rhythmic, begin to build.*)

…good come good come come come good come good come come come. Good. Come…good come good come come come good come good come come come. Good. Come…good come good come come come good come good come come come. Good. Come…

(*Gradually the fit leaves TRAINERS. LEX is quiet. TRAINERS stares up at her, her eyes swimming. She reaches out, smiling.*)

TRAIN: Lex…

(*For a moment, LEX stares at TRAINERS' hand, tempted to*

hold it. She backs away.)

LEX: You need a fucking... (*She gets out her mobile, rings a number.*) Yeah, ambulance... I don't know...it was like a fit... Twenty-six...Harnall Lane... Trainers. Yeah, that's her name... I don't know, I don't know her last name... Yeah, I'll wait... (*She rings off.*) I'll wait...

(*Silence. SHELLEY prepares LEX's dinner.*)

SHELL: You thought about what you're doing for Christmas, yet? No doubt you'll turn up on the doorstep... Sometimes, it'd be good if you could just ring me, you know what I'm saying? Do you eat sausages? You turned veggie yet? Or is it peas?...are you against people eating peas...?

(*Music plays.*)

5

LEX's flat. 9.05pm.

ADDY and LORNA are still at the table. The pen and paper still between them. LORNA chews on the remnants of the roll she had earlier. LEX sits across from them, silent. Until.

LEX: Did you do the counts?

(*Beat.*)

ADDY: You know we did.

(*LORNA avoids LEX's stare, moves to another part of the room. ADDY nods at the plaster on LEX's hand.*)

You alright with that?

(*Long silence.*)

How bad was it...? This thing on the train.

(*No answer. Long silence.*)

You okay?

(*Silence.*)

Where you been?

(*Beat.*)

LEX: Shell's. (*Beat.*) Listen, we need to get sorted. Get some new hits organised.

ADDY: Yeah?

LEX: You need to get onto it. Tell Lorna to get her head together.

ADDY: Lex, / listen…

LEX: I don't want things stopping.

> (*She stares at him, his protest quelled as soon as it's begun. She looks at the light switch.*)

How many did you do?

ADDY: One thousand, two hundred. There's no one coming within a hundred feet, yeah?

> (*The doorbell rings. RUEBEN is at the door.*)

RUBE: Lex…open the door. Lex… I want to talk to you…

> (*Silence.*)

Lex…… Come on, open up…

> (*ADDY goes to the door, shouting through.*)

ADDY: What do you want?

RUBE: I want to speak to Lex.

ADDY: Well she doesn't want to speak to you, so fuck off.

RUBE: *Listen*, she put Trainers in hospital. Okay? She beat up your mate, and I want to talk to her.

ADDY: When?

RUBE: I don't know when… But I want to find out what's been going on.

ADDY: Why would she want to talk to you?

RUBE: Addy…is it Addy? …Look, I'm not the police, I work with people like Lex, people like yourself, I do it all the time. Yeah?

> (*Pause. ADDY opens the door. RUBE comes in. LEX is looking at her shoes, lining the toe ends up so that they are dead dead in line, when she fails she scuffs her feet like she is rubbing out the last attempt and then starts again. RUBE takes out a handkerchief, wipes sweat slowly from his upper lip. Eventually…*)

Why did you beat up Trainers?

> (*Silence.*)

LEX: What?

RUBE: I said: *why* did you beat up Trainers? (*Beat.*) Why's that girl got to spend the next few weeks putting up with some dentist deciding which teeth she can keep and which teeth got so smashed up that they're no use to anyone apart from some old aged pensioner who can't afford her own set of false teeth?

LORNA: Which dentist did she go to?

RUBE: Do you think it's a joke?

LORNA: No.

RUBE: Is it funny her lying there now while they're scanning her head, worrying over her because she's gone so soggy and white she can hardly make her breath come out straight?

LORNA: Is she alright?

RUBE: *No*...she's not.

(*Silence.*)

Why did you do it?

LEX: Payback.

RUBE: What?

LEX: Payback.

RUBE: No, that's not payback, that's vicious. (*Beat.*) Trainers isn't going to hurt you.

LEX: No.

RUBE: You'll get custody for this.

LEX: That's up to Trainers.

RUBE: Not just her. I'm obliged to contact the police.

ADDY: No chance, you're not saying a fucking word.

LORNA: (*To ADDY.*) You got a can for Rueben? (*To RUBE.*) You want a drink of beer?

RUBE: *What?*

LORNA: I said, you want a drink of beer?

RUBE: What? No. (*To LEX.*) At the end of the day, you'll probably get away with it.

LEX: Yeah?

RUBE: Yeah, because she acts like you're something to look up to. I'm sitting there in the hospital and she's like, 'Lex this, Lex that'. And him: 'She doesn't want to talk to you...' People acting all the time like you're something special, like there's no one going to answer you back.

LEX: That's because no one can tell me anything.

RUBE: Yeah? How's that?

LEX: Listen, they're here with me because they want to be.

(*Long long silence.*)

RUBE: So what about Trainers?

LEX: I'll send her a get well card.

RUBE: No. Something more. You need to go back on all this, you need to go back in your mind, see her lying there.

ADDY: Jesus, this is doing my fucking head in. Listen, she panned Trainers cos she got too gobby, alright? (*He leans over RUBE.*) *Alright?*
(*Silence.*)

RUBE: Whatever you say.

ADDY: Yeah, well I'm saying. (*Pause. To LEX.*) Might get some chips; you want me to stay or...?

LEX: No. He doesn't bother me.

ADDY: You getting anything?

LORNA: Might have a burger. (*To RUBE.*) You want a burger?

LEX: Lorna...
(*LORNA gets the pen and paper from the table. She looks at RUBE, like she might see something in him that can help her. Thinks again. LORNA goes, followed by ADDY.*
Long silence.)

RUBE: People are getting sick and tired of you, you know that?
(*No answer.*)
You and your 'crew', messing up the town. Thousands of pounds' worth of damage.
(*Silence.*)
It's a mess.
(*Pause.*)
What you did to Trainers.
(*Long long silence. He goes to her.*)
(*Quiet.*) How did you do it?

LEX: What?

RUBE: I wanted to know.

LEX: What you on about?

RUBE: Fist? A tool? What did you use to make such a mess of her...?

LEX: Why?
(*Silence. He stays close to her.*)

RUBE: What do you think about?

LEX: What?

RUBE: When you're beating the shit out of someone? What do you think about?

LEX: How the fuck do I know? I just think about getting the job done, getting away fast as I can.
(*Pause.*)
What you asking me all this for?
(*Long silence.*)

RUBE: You're breaking apart.
(*Silence.*)

LEX: I want you to go now, yeah?
(*Long silence.*)

RUBE: Let me have a look.

LEX: What at?

RUBE: Your photos. Trainers told me you keep records of all the hits you do: dates, times, streets.

LEX: Alright, I give in, what's the game?

RUBE: What game?

LEX: The game you're playing with me.

RUBE: I'm not playing any games.

LEX: Yes you are. I don't know what you want with me but I don't mix with do gooders and fucking mind warpers, makes me sweat, you know what I'm saying?
(*Pause.*)

RUBE: Let me see.
(*RUBE holds out his hand. LEX stares at him. She gets a photo album. RUBE flicks through them.*)

LEX: Slow down, you're supposed to appreciate the art.

RUBE: I am appreciating it, I just can't read / any of it. What's it say?

LEX: You cheeky fucking...you're not supposed to read it.

RUBE: So why spray stuff on a wall if you don't want anyone to understand it? (*He looks again at the photos.*) Who did this?

LEX: Addy.

RUBE: You mean he beat this guy up like that, and then someone took a photo of him?

LEX: Yeah.

RUBE: Jesus. (*He throws the book down.*) Beating someone up isn't something to gloat about.

LEX: Slow / down.

RUBE: I could walk out of here now and I could ring the police, / I could get you and your mates picked up.

LEX: Listen, don't walk into my house and start fucking pushing at me.

(*Silence.*)

So why don't you?

(*Silence. LEX puts the photos back in a folder. RUBE watches her, transfixed.*)

RUBE: The next hit you do, I want to come out with you.

LEX: What?! / You just fucking…

RUBE: Why not?

LEX: Because you're a twat, because you couldn't mug / a mug of fucking coffee.

(*RUBE feigns a punch towards her, she is instinctive and lashes out in defence.*)

What you doing…?

RUBE: I was the best fighter in my street, honest. (*He feigns another punch and she pushes him back.*) I was just mucking about, it's alright to enjoy yourself now and then, people do it all the time.

LEX: Yeah? Well I don't get it. You give me all that shit about Trainers and now you want to come out with us and do exactly the same thing. I don't get that, that's being a hypocrite, yeah? Is that what you are? Are you just another fucking bullshit merchant I got to manoeuvre my way around?

(*Pause.*)

RUBE: You think that's what I'm about?

(*Pause.*)

LEX: I ain't got a fucking clue what you're about.

(*Music plays.*)

6

Wednesday, 4:55pm.

Music plays.

In LEX's flat, LEX lays a map out on the table. LORNA and ADDY watch.

As this happens, TRAINERS, in a hospital gown, looks at her face in a hand mirror, touching the cuts, the bruising.

TRAIN: ...yumlike, you left me dying...now I got the docs fussing...yumlike, now I'm not dying...now I'm smiling, yeah? Cos of what I found, cos of what you showed me... Hard head, honey face girl...yumlike Lex, still my friend...yumlike, after everything you just done to me...yumlike, why didn't it stay just you and me...? yumlike, how did stuff get so bad between us...?
(Pause.)

LEX: Go through the new hit.
(Silence.)
Lorna...

LORNA: I don't think it's a good idea, yeah?

LEX: What isn't?

LORNA: Going back out so soon; after the boy, after the train...

LEX: Did you hear anything yet?

LORNA: I've been in my room all day.

LEX: What?

LORNA: I said, I've been in my room all day.

LEX: Right. So just go through it.
(The doorbell rings. ADDY goes out to answer it. LEX stares at LORNA, LORNA stares at the floor. ADDY returns with RUBE.)

ADDY: Seen what the cat dragged in.
(LEX looks at RUBE, waits.)

LEX: What do you want? I'm busy.

RUBE: Yeah.
(Silence.)

LEX: So?

RUBE: I just… I wanted to see you.

LEX: About what?

RUBE: Nothing… Just…

(*Silence. RUBE watches LEX.*)

ADDY: (*To LEX.*) You want me to twat him?

(*LEX watches RUBE, like she is trying to summon the energy to take control. Eventually…*)

LEX: Leave him. I can't be bothered with him. (*Beat.*) Lorna.

ADDY: I'll do it.

LEX: No, I want her to do it.

(*Reluctantly, LORNA starts, warming up as she gets into her stride.*)

LORNA: We get the number forty bus and we go all the way into town, we don't get off at the first stop, we get off after the ring road and go down the gravel path towards / the post office.

LEX: What's important about the gravel path?

LORNA: There's two gravel paths and it's the one on the left going towards the undertakers. There's a flight of iron stairs that goes back over the ring road…

RUBE: Can you get her to slow down?

ADDY: (*To RUEBEN.*) Eh!

(*ADDY puts a finger to his mouth. LORNA carries on as before.*)

LORNA: The iron stairs that go back over the ring road've got these big girders that run right across it. The paint'll go on really neat…

RUBE: I still can't hear you…

LORNA: *Shut up twat.*

RUBE: What?

ADDY: Shut it.

LORNA: When we're on the iron bridge we get the banner that Trainers made, it's got sixteen different colours and says 'Check us out' in massive fucking letters.

RUBE: 'Check us out'?

LORNA: Yeah. 'Check us out.' We unravel the / banner and…

RUBE: What does that mean then?

LORNA: It's a catch phrase.

RUBE: A what?

LORNA: Trainers said you don't give the game away. Like, people see it and wonder what it means, 'Check Us Out', and all the time it's going into their heads; next time you do another catch phrase and it's something like, 'We're checking you out'...

RUBE: Yeah?

LORNA: ...it slips into people's heads. Trainers says it's a whispering campaign, like '118 118'.

RUBE: So what is it you're selling?

LORNA: No one's selling anything.

RUBE: So why do you need a catchphrase?

LORNA: (*To LEX.*) You told me to go through it yeah...?!!
    (*LORNA retreats to a corner of the room. Silence. Until...*)

ADDY: (*To LEX.*) What hits we doing exactly?

LEX: I gave yous all a list.

ADDY: I know you did, / I lost it.

LEX: Fuck's sake. (*Pause.*) Nat West, Lloyds and all the cash points on Rowett Street, all the post boxes outside the Co-op, the Athena, the Jaguar and The Crown; all the phone boxes on the other side of the road, the doors of the Chamber of Commerce and the side wall of the Town Hall. If you see anyone, you pan them, wallets, money, mobiles, the works. (*Beat.*) I got to go and see someone now, yeah? So we'll meet by the market, seven o'clock. (*Pause.*) What's the problem?
    (*Pause.*)

ADDY: Nothing. And what about numbnuts? What's he doing?

LEX: He's coming with us.

ADDY: *What?* / how come?

LEX: Cos he asked if he could, if he gets caught then that's his own fucking problem, maybe it'll teach him a lesson.

ADDY: Yeah? and how do we know he won't go blabbing to the Five O?

LEX: Because he won't. Because there won't be any Five O to blab to. We can't get caught. There's nothing big

enough to stop us.
(*Music plays.*)

7

In the hospital, 6:00pm.

Music plays. LEX visits TRAINERS. TRAINERS lifts her hand, reaches out to LEX, pulling her down so she can whisper in her ear.

TRAIN: ...magic... (*She nods.*) yumlike...
   (*As this happens, the music starts to grow, starts to pound as LEX absorbs the meaning of the word, the pressure of it becoming too much for her, until...*)

8

LEX's kitchen and SHELLEY's house, 7:35pm.

Music playing, the sound of ADDY screaming in pain as he comes piling into the kitchen, RUEBEN and LORNA are close behind.

LEX legs it into SHELLEY's house and locks herself in the bathroom.

ADDY: Aaaaaaaaaaaaaaaaaahhhhhhhhhhhhhh!!!!!
LORNA: ...get something for a cloth...!
ADDY: Not my black shirt... / that's my black shirt!
LORNA: Careful.
ADDY: *Fuck...*
RUBE: Wriggle your fingers. / Rotate your wrist.
ADDY: What?
RUBE: Just wave.
ADDY: What do you mean just wave?
LORNA: We could put some cream on it, antiseptic.
ADDY: Antiseptic's no good, it's fucking acid, yeah?
LORNA: Yeah.
   (*Pause.*)
RUBE: Where did Lex go?
ADDY: Are you stupid, or something?
LORNA: She fucked off.

ADDY: Yeah. And where the fuck were you? She does a fucking runner, and five minutes later we get jumped by a van load of Five O and some fucking mob from the council cleaning division. Some fat bastard leaps out from the wheelie bin next to me and suddenly there's two, three, four, there's six of them; these fat fucking council cleaners chasing us down Rowett Street like they're all on twenty grand bonuses... (*Beat. He looks at his arm.*) Acid's made it all go bubbly...

RUBE: It's not acid.

ADDY: How do you know? How do you know the council haven't just started using acid the last few days?

RUBE: Because they'd have cleaning agents with them.

LORNA: Why?

ADDY: Because acid don't clean graffiti off.

RUBE: Right.

LORNA: So how come they're still carrying the stuff?

ADDY: *They're not, / they weren't!*

LORNA: Don't shout at me twat!

ADDY: Well we already established they don't use acid to clean graffiti off, so I'm saying /...

LORNA: Yeah, I know / what you're saying...

ADDY: No you don't know what I'm saying, what I'm / saying is.

LORNA: Yeah, I know, I know what / you're saying.

ADDY: No, you don't know / what I'm saying.

LORNA: I / do...

RUBE: You / don't...

ADDY: I'm saying that I've got something on my arm but it's not acid...

LORNA: You're saying that you've got something on your arm but it's not acid...

RUBE: He's saying that he's got something on his arm, but it's not acid.

LORNA: ...I know, but it's not acid...

(*Beat.*)

I know.

(*Beat.*)

ADDY: Your last name Einstein?

LORNA: Fuck off.

> (*The action cuts to LEX and SHELLEY. LEX is in the bathroom.*)

LEX: Shelley...

SHELL: What's going on?

LEX: Got to hide...

SHELL: Who from...?.

LEX: ...*her*...what she said...

SHELL: What?

LEX: What she said...

SHELL: Who?

LEX: What she said...blood's going round me and I can't fucking do it...

SHELL: Do what?

LEX: The hit. Tonight. I can't do it, I've got the can and I'm spraying...everytime I'm spraying, I'm crying, and my legs are carrying me, they're fucking...and there's this there's this there's this this this...

SHELL: This what?...

LEX: I don't know, the thing, the thing, the whoosh thing when I always know it's going to be bad come bad come, when the thing...this this this...when it runs through me, when I know I'll love it and when I know I'll hate it, but tonight, first time, I'm *scared* what I might do Shell...

SHELL: What the fuck're you talking about...?

> (*Beat.*)

LEX: What she said.

ADDY: What you doing?

SHELL: What who said?

LORNA: What do / you think...?

SHELL: Lex, will you just come / out?

ADDY: Yeah I know, but you can't go leaving now, the police could be anywhere.

LORNA: I can, I told you. That's why I want to go...

SHELL: Lex.

LORNA: (*To RUBE.*) You got a settee I can sleep on?

RUBE: What for?

LORNA: Cos I'm scared.

SHELL: Come on.

ADDY: No she's not, she's not scared of nothing. Me, Lorna, we live here with Lex, yeah? She tells us what she wants and we do it. It works. There's nothing to be scared of.

LORNA: Yeah, that's right, we do the counts, we do what *Lex* says...

SHELL: What who said...?

LORNA: I do the blinds, Trainers stamps, Addy does the lights.

LEX: Trainers.

RUBE: He does the what?

LORNA: The lights.

SHELL: Trainers?

LORNA: Twelve hundred every day. Lex's orders.

LEX: Yeah.

RUBE: Why?

LORNA: So people know to stay away. Lex's idea.

ADDY: No, *my* idea, she just took it and fucked it up.

SHELL: What did she say?

ADDY: I did it for you...the lights... (*To RUBE.*) When Lorna first arrived, so she could find her way back over the park... (*To LORNA.*) ...so I knew you'd come back... (*Packing food and clothes into her bag, LORNA stops suddenly; looks at ADDY.*)

SHELL: What did Trainers say? ...Look, just come out and I'll give you a cuddle, yeah?
(*Beat.*)

LORNA: Yeah.

SHELL: You want a cuddle...? (*Pause.*) Lex?
(*No answer. Silence. SHELLEY slumps against the door. She counts the fags left in her packet, under her breath. In the hospital, slowly, TRAINERS pulls herself out of bed. As she speaks, she packs her bag. LORNA has the pen and paper and moves towards RUBE.*)

TRAIN: ...yumlike I got this friend...yumlike she put my big blood on the carpet, her punches and my big blood, like a sea...

LORNA: I was going to ask you the other day.

RUBE: Pardon?

TRAIN: ...I found out what you got Lex...

LORNA: I was going to ask you.

TRAIN: ...yumlike, yesterday, I seen it...

RUBE: (*To ADDY.*) What's she saying...?

TRAIN: ...felt it...all these years when I never seen it...

LORNA: I asked Addy and he won't help me.

SHELL: Lex...

LORNA: I really need something writing. Like words, for saying sorry and stuff.

TRAIN: ...yumlike, now I got to see it again, got to feel it again...

LORNA: When I was fifteen I ran away from home.

TRAIN: ...yumlike, I got to.

LORNA: I come from Bristol, yeah? Do you know Bristol?

RUBE: Pardon?

LORNA: When I'm on the coach it's alright. I've got an auntie lives in Burnley. I get to her address and she's moved. Three years by myself, but now I've had enough.

SHELL: You just going to ignore me?

RUBE: What is it you want me to write?

ADDY: She doesn't want you to write anything. Look, she rang them. Six months ago. We were going to go and see her parents, and they told her she couldn't ever come back, / not unless she rang again and formally apologised...

LORNA: Fuck off.

ADDY: It's true...*formally* apologised...for what she did to them. Jesus, you don't hear from your kid for three years and then they want to come home, what do you do? You just open your arms, yeah?

RUBE: But she wants to go home, Addy she wants her mum and dad.

ADDY: Yeah, but they don't want her...I know it... (*Pause.*) They never do.

SHELL: What we going to do Lex?

(*Pause.*)

RUBE: (*To LORNA.*) What do you want me to say?

(*LORNA gives RUBE the pen and paper. SHELLEY takes half of a torn photo from her pocket, holds it up to look at it.*)

LORNA: Just write down some...like some words, for when I'm on the phone... When I get nervous, I can't... Can you just give me some ideas, some words...?

(*Music plays. Whilst RUBE writes and LORNA dictates to him, LEX watches edgily as SHELLEY slides the half torn side of the photograph under the bathroom door.*)

LEX: ...what you doing?

SHELL: You remember the first time they split us up, when I went to live with those people in Bolton...? Thought I'd never see you again...

LEX: Yeah, well you did.

SHELL: I know, too fucking right I did. I tore it in half, yeah? ...Half for you, half for me... Where's your half?

LEX: Not now Shell...just leave it.

SHELL: *Where's* your half?

LEX: You want me to scream the house down?

(*RUBE gives the pen and paper back to LORNA.*)

LORNA: Thanks.

RUBE: Alright. Have you got Lex's mobile number?

LEX: Raaaaaaaaaaaaaaaaaaaaaaaaaaaaaaaaaaaaaa!!!

SHELL: Stop it!...what the fuck's wrong with you??... I'm just, I'm asking you... Stop it!!!!

(*LEX's mobile starts ringing.*)

Lex...?

(*Silence. Just the mobile ringing.*)

Is that your mobile...? (*No answer.*) Lex...?

(*The mobile is in LEX's trackie top on the kitchen table. SHELLEY answers it.*)

Hello.

RUBE: Lex...?

SHELL: No, Shelley, her sister. Who's calling? / Listen, you've called at a really bad time, yeah?

RUBE: It's Rueben...I'm a... (*Beat.*) I work for social services... Where's Lex then?...can I ask, is she alright?...

SHELL: No she's not, she's hysterical.

RUBE: I was with her tonight / and then she just disappeared.

SHELL: What happened?... Social services?

RUBE: I don't know. Yeah... That's what I want to find out. Can I come and see her, / where do you live?

SHELL: Hold on, wait a minute, I don't even know you. I've got kids in bed and stuff.

RUBE: It'll be alright. I told you, she knows me, she knows who I am. If I come round, I'll explain. You don't have to let me in. Is that okay?... I'll just talk to her...
(*Music plays.*)

9

SHELLEY's house, 8:20pm.

RUBE offers to shake SHELLEY's hand. SHELLEY refuses.

RUBE: Rueben.
(*Beat.*)

SHELL: Right.

RUBE: How is she?
(*Beat.*)

SHELL: Sorry, but I didn't think she was...What you were saying on the phone, I thought social services gave up on her.
(*Pause.*)

RUBE: No, we... (*Pause.*) I mean...

SHELL: Are you her social worker?
(*Beat.*)

RUBE: Yeah... Well she's not on my case load as such, but it's just we have a policy, you know? We track people, we keep a watch.

SHELL: She didn't say.

RUBE: How often does she tell you anything?

SHELL: Never. One minute she's living here with me, the next she's moving out again...

RUBE: You said she was... Sorry, is it Shelley?
(*SHELLEY nods.*)

Did you say she was hysterical Shelley? / When we
spoke on the phone.

SHELL: Yeah, I don't know...she just came running in,
babbling on about something. I think one of her friends
said something to upset her...

(*RUBE waits. Eventually...*)

SHELL: She's in the bathroom.

(*Pause.*)

RUBE: (*Calling.*) Lex?

(*Pause.*)

LEX: What do you want?

RUBE: I want to see you.

LEX: Fucking clingon.

RUBE: I was worried.

LEX: You don't have to bother with me, yeah? / You're the
one invited yourself into all this.

RUBE: Yeah, but that's the point... I do have to bother.

(*Beat.*)

LEX: What you on about?

SHELL: Just open up, yeah?

(*Silence.*)

Right, so I'll break the door down.

LEX: You won't.

SHELL: Watch me.

LEX: Just fucking... I'm coming alright?

(*Slowly, LEX opens the door. SHELLEY moves forward,
RUBE signals to her to wait. Pause.*)

RUBE: What happened?

(*Pause.*)

SHELL: Why you crying?

LEX: I just went to see Trainers. It's no big deal.

(*Silence.*)

RUBE: And?

LEX: And nothing. Why should I tell you? I don't even
know you.

SHELL: So tell me... How'd you get in such a state...?

LEX: Don't know.

SHELL: Right.

LEX: Fuck's sake... Look, I just went to visit Trainers in hospital, alright? Before the hit and stuff. When I beat her up the other day, she had this fit...she was frothing and things, and I started whispering to her:...good come good come come come good come good come come come...

RUBE: What's that?

LEX: I made it up. (*Pause.*) Sometimes stuff happens to me...like I go off on one, yeah? Like I see someone, something, and my fucking temper just...and I get these words coming, and then there's like this whoosh thing...like I'm going... (*She points her hand upwards.*) and I know I can like, look away, or I can really go for it. Yeah? (*She stops.*) It doesn't matter.
(*She goes for the door. As the scene continues, TRAINERS appears in the hospital, in her gown, as LEX remembers last seeing her.*)

RUBE: Finish what you were saying.

LEX: I forgot.

RUBE: When you beat up Trainers, she had a fit.

LEX: Yeah, but then it passed, like someone turned off the gas.

RUBE: Fits can pass quickly.

LEX: I know. (*Beat.*) But this was like *I* made it stop. I beat the fuck out of her, yeah? But then after, I've got the words coming...

TRAIN: ...good come, good come...

LEX: ...and I've got that fucking whoosh thing, yeah? But now it feels soft... I'm soothing her, stroking her head. And so I'm like, how come one minute I was beating the fuck out of someone, and now the next I'm doing the opposite? I reckon I could carry on, like it didn't happen, you know what I'm saying? It's just tonight Trainers asks me how I did it, and I'm like... 'Trainers, I don't want to talk about it. I just come to say sorry and stuff...' but she keeps on, she says...

TRAIN: ...yumlike, all that 'good come' stuff, the whispering, it was like a spell.

LEX: I says: 'Don't be stupid, it ain't no fucking spell...'
...so then she starts again:

TRAIN: ...yumlike, you and me, we been together
ages...yumlike, I never knew you had something like
that...

LEX: 'Like what...?'
(*Silence.*)
And that's how I got so fucked up. She pulls me down to
her, whispers in my ear... What she said, yeah? what she
called it and stuff. It's in my head.

SHELL: What did Trainers say?... What did she call it?
(*Pause.*)

LEX: Magic.
(*She is staring at SHELLEY. Looks back to RUBE.*)
Like my dad. He used to make things disappear, did
tricks. He could make my mum disappear.

RUBE: Yeah?

LEX: Bed times. My dad and my mum. (*To SHELLEY.*)
Sometimes they used to sing to us.

SHELL: 'Me and My Shadow.'

LEX: Yeah... (*As the memory spreads, LEX goes more and more
into herself.*) They'd be singing, and they'd just be dead
happy, the two of them, they'd just be so fucking happy
and we'd be laughing, and on the inside I'd be
whispering to myself, 'It's alright, cos tonight we're in
between...'

RUBE: Between?

LEX: The fighting. For a few days it's been good...
(*Whispering again.*) '...tonight it's alright, cos tonight
we're in between...tonight it's alright, cos tonight we're
in between...', and I'd come alive with all that fucking
love I could feel. Yeah?... Love like the ironing board,
the love we got in the cooker, the fridge, love like the
shoe cupboard. So much love filling our house. And I'm
so happy...They'd be singing away, and then they'd get
to the finale bit, and dad would make mum disappear.
(*Beat.*)

RUBE: How?

LEX: Don't matter how, she just...and he does this...
> (*She holds up both hands, wriggles her fingers and clicks them.*)

...and he twists a bit and she's gone. Then he'd switch off the light, and he'd say 'God bless'.

SHELL: 'God bless.'

LEX: Magic dad. Magic hands, magic fingers.
> (*Silence.*)

Then it's back to normal, and he's beating the fuck out of mum... But now it's gone further, yeah? she's really bleeding and stuff, like her nose is broken, and he chases me and Shell, up the stairs...gets his hand round the bathroom door. His fingers, magic fingers, magic's winning, and then we're like...wham! and he screams and we're running again. First time ever, he starts punching us, tries to strangle me... (*Pause.*) 'The Big Bad Bastard'... 'The Evil Fingered Magician.'
> (*LEX and SHELLEY watch each other.*)

After that, everything's different, magic dad stops the tricks. All magic's bad magic.
> (*Silence.*)

He's dead now.

RUBE: Where's your mum?

LEX: I don't know. Shell keeps in touch now and then.
> (*Beat.*) But we all loved each other, yeah?
> (*Beat.*)

SHELL: Yeah.

LEX: (*To RUBE.*) We did.

RUBE: I believe you.

LEX: In between...
> (*LEX stops, sways. She makes a noise like air is escaping and then faints. RUBE breaks her fall, holds her. Silence, until...*)

SHELL: Lex...?

RUBE: Give her a sec...
> (*SHELLEY and RUBE watch each other, music plays and RUBE lifts LEX up. He carries her upstairs, SHELLEY leading the way.*
> *As the music plays, RUBE returns and sits, waits. He takes*

out a note book and sketches quickly, edgy. SHELLEY returns.)
  She alright?
SHELL: Asleep... *(Pause.)* Sorry, you need to get off.
RUBE: I don't mind. *(Silence.)* Does she faint a lot?
SHELL: She did as a kid.
RUBE: I think she forgets to breathe... I see it all the time.
  I get kids blacking out in front of me, they get so
  worked up, all that anger, and they're like...
  *(He holds his breath, inflates his cheeks. It makes SHELLEY
  smile. Silence.)*
  How does it feel when she talks about your family like
  that? *(Pause.)* Don't worry so much. Things get better.
SHELL: Yeah?
RUBE: I can... I mean I explained earlier, she's not exactly
  under my... But I can try and help her.
SHELL: You don't have to.
RUBE: I know I don't. But if it's what you want.
SHELL: How?
RUBE: Change of scenery. I've got quite a big flat, it's a
  great view, right over towards the station, out towards
  the river. Save you the hassle tonight. You look
  exhausted... I can try and have a word with her. I don't
  know, it might be better, like it's not so official.
SHELL: I can't see you getting through to her.
RUBE: Well, no. Whatever you want.
  (Silence.)
  What I can do Shelley, is this... *(He starts to write in his
  notebook.)* Why don't we get the three of us over to my
  flat. I'll give you my number, alright? *(He writes the
  number down, rips the page out of the notebook.)* You can see
  her in, and then I'll ring you in the morning, and you
  can come over and pick her up.
  *(SHELLEY stares at the number on the paper. RUBE hands
  it to her.)*
  What do you think?
  (Music plays.)

10

LEX's flat, 8:40pm.

ADDY is alone. He stands by the light switch, does his counts: lights on, off, on, off, taptap, taptap. LORNA enters, with a rucksack. She has the evening paper.

LORNA: CCTV...
    (*ADDY looks at the paper.*)
LORNA: Lex. Trainers. Me... They'll be looking for us.
ADDY: Yeah.
LORNA: You think that's alright?
ADDY: The boy didn't *die*, yeah? You didn't kill no one.
LORNA: What's the fucking difference?
ADDY: Look, I know what you're going to say. But what if we stay...? I don't mean stay here, we'll leave, like you've been wanting, but we'll keep it just me and you, no one else. We'll find somewhere new...we'll...
LORNA: No... (*Pause.*) Addy, I might be going home.
    (*Silence.*)
ADDY: Did you ring them?
    (*She nods.*)
    What did they say?
LORNA: They said they'd come and get me. Take me back.
ADDY: Where from?
LORNA: The bus station. Eleven o'clock tomorrow morning.
ADDY: Just like that?!
LORNA: What's so funny...?
ADDY: How do you know they'll come...?
LORNA: They *will*... They will... And dad'll want to buy me a custard doughnut, or something, and mum'll be wanting to get off, beat the weekend traffic.
ADDY: Yeah?
    (*Beat.*)
LORNA: Yeah.
    (*Silence. She gets up, does up the buttons on her coat, he helps her, she touches his hand away. He moves instead to her collar,*

straightening, setting the collar straight. She eases him off.
It's like watching a rhythm.)
Come with me.

ADDY: No.

LORNA: I was going to sleep rough somewhere. It's only a
night...

ADDY: What?

LORNA: I said, I was going to sleep rough somewhere. It's
only a night.

ADDY: No. Look, you just go... Meet them by yourself,
yeah?

LORNA: Ads...

ADDY: Yeah. It's better on your own. (*Beat.*) When you're
settled and stuff...ring me.
(*LORNA goes. Music plays. Lost, ADDY looks around the
empty room. Hanging onto the rituals he trusts, he starts
again at the light switch, goes to the window, twists the
Venetian blinds, open, closed, open, closed. Goes back to the
light switch, on, off, on, off, goes back to the blinds, goes back
to the light switch. This continues, as the action crosses to...*)

11

RUBE's flat, 8:45pm.

*RUBE carries LEX to a sofa bed. He puts her down and he and
SHELLEY stand over her. LEX is fast asleep.*

SHELL: You reckon it's alright?

RUBE: How much do you want this to work?

SHELL: I don't know... (*Beat.*) It's a lot; for you.

RUBE: It's my choice.

SHELL: Is it something we can do?

RUBE: If we agree, then it is.

SHELL: I can't just give up on her, can I?... I worry like
she'll get herself banged up somewhere, like one day
she'll really go and do something.
(*Silence.*)
I'll ring you.

(*She goes. Pause. RUBE looks back at LEX and then puts the key in the door. He turns it and locks it, putting the key in his pocket.*
Music plays.)

12

Thursday. In the street. 1:00pm.

The sound of heavy rain. LORNA stands with her hood pulled up, shoulders hunched against the rain. She eats a bag of chips, watches, watches.

A soundscape of the life of the street can be heard. She screws the chips up, lowers to her haunches. Crouches. Watches.

This happens whilst:

13

1:05pm. In RUBE's flat, LEX still sleeps.

In LEX's flat, ADDY stands by the lights, his arm arching behind his head so he rests his finger on the light switch. It is as if he hasn't moved for days. A still life painting bathed in the richness of the winter light. The doorbell rings. He doesn't move. It rings again. He goes to answer it, returns with TRAINERS.

TRAIN: ...yumlike, where is everyone...?
(*No answer.*)
You seen Lex?
ADDY: I haven't seen anyone Trainers, alright? Monday the house is full, now I'm the houseguard, just me and the counts. I do the blinds, I do the light switch, I'm knackered, but I'm keeping it going.
TRAIN: ...yumlike you alright? Where's Lorna?
(*No answer.*)
...yumlike I been in the hospital.
ADDY: I heard...so what you doing out? You look fucking terrible...

(*ADDY throws the paper at TRAINERS, shows her the CCTV picture.*)

Nice photo, by the way. (*Beat.*) She rang her folks last night, went to meet them this morning... She was going to ring me... You want tea?

TRAIN: (*Reading the paper.*) ...fuck...

ADDY: Can't get out the door to go for a piss. (*ADDY stares into the tin.*) Got no tea. You want anything else?

TRAIN: ...yumlike, so where's Lex?

ADDY: Gone as well.

TRAIN: What?...

ADDY: You deaf.

TRAIN: ...you mean she just fucked off on me?

ADDY: I didn't say that.

TRAIN: ...she can't...

ADDY: Did she do that to your teeth?

TRAIN: ...I need to find her...

ADDY: Hold on...don't go for a bit, yeah...?

(*He holds TRAINERS by the arm.*)

Do your counts with me.

TRAIN: ...I haven't done them for days.

ADDY: Just for a bit... *Please.*

(*Pause.*)

TRAIN: ...yum...

ADDY: Please.

(*ADDY is at the light switch, he starts flicking it; on, off, on, off, nodding at TRAINERS to start her ritual. Reluctantly, she starts to stamp in rhythm with ADDY. This goes on; the lights on and off, the stamping on the floorboard, ADDY watching TRAINERS. Lights on, lights off, stamp, stamp. Lights on, lights off, stamp, stamp. It is a compelling rhythm that they build up. They watch each other as the rhythm drives on, until eventually, pulling herself back to real time, TRAINERS stops. ADDY stops also, and she goes to him, puts her hand on the light switch to stop him.*)

TRAIN: ...yumlike, you don't have to do it.

(*ADDY's face creases, TRAINERS goes, and ADDY moves to the blinds, begins to open and close them.*
Music plays.)

14

RUBE's house, 1:30pm.

LEX is still asleep. RUBE is there. LEX jumps out of her sleep, freaked.

RUBE: It's alright.
    (*Pause.*)
    You've slept right through the morning.
    (*Pause.*)
    Last night we had a bit of a chat, at Shelley's…? (*Beat.*)
    Then you fainted. Me and your sister agreed you needed
    a break from all the pressure you've been putting on
    yourself. So we decided you'd come and stay with me.
    No distractions.
    (*Beat.*)
LEX: What?
RUBE: Hot running water; sunny view.
    (*Beat.*)
LEX: You're a nutter…
RUBE: I just offered to help. You got yourself worked up,
    you fainted. Woke up in the taxi. Fainted again. I bet you
    don't eat, do you eat?
LEX: Everyone eats.
RUBE: Yeah, but there's eating, and there's *eating*. No
    wonder you're going round fainting all the time.
LEX: I don't faint.
RUBE: You do. (*Beat.*) I'll make you something.
    (*As the next section unfolds, RUBE goes to a cupboard. He*
    takes out bananas, a knife, Angel Delight mix. Pours water
    into a tea pot.)
LEX: I need to get back
RUBE: To your 'crew'?… I always hate that word. What
    good words are there to describe a group of young
    people on the make? Posse? Gang?
LEX: Where are we?
RUBE: I told you.
LEX: I mean what part of town?

RUBE: You hungry?

LEX: Just tell me.

RUBE: South. (*Beat.*) I don't actually think your crew'll be there. I can't see you all staying together much longer.

LEX: They'll be there.

RUBE: How long you been together?

LEX: What?

RUBE: You can't be together forever... You've already lost Trainers. Doesn't take much working out. Young people lose interest easily; loyalties, especially in / the sort of circles you move in...

LEX: What do you know about loyalties...? Fuck's sake, Trainers found Addy in a bus shelter, alright? Covered in sick, three day old hard sick down his shirt, like he'd tried to top himself. And I saved Trainers a million times in care, whenever some bitch was about to plaster her all over the wall. So we got loyalties, yeah? (*Beat.*) Only, I don't need anyone to be loyal. (*Pause.*) I just...if they want to stay, do what I ask them...then that's the way we get along. (*Pause.*) How the fuck did I get to meet you?

RUBE: Forgotten already?

LEX: You're a bit...

RUBE: What? I'm alright me.

(*His phone rings.*)

Just a sec... I made some tea... Hello?

TRAIN: ...yumlike, it's me.

RUBE: Alright. (*Beat.*) Listen, I can't really talk at the moment.

TRAIN: ...you seen Lex?

(*He looks to LEX who is pouring tea from the pot.*)

RUBE: No. Why?

TRAIN: ...I didn't know if you'd seen her, she's not answering her mobile...yumlike I need to find her yeah? I got stuff planned...yumlike, she's got the magic...

RUBE: What? You alright?

TRAIN: ...yumlike not really...I got involved in a fuck up and stuff...

RUBE: Like what?

TRAIN: ...yumlike, Lex smashed some lad over the head on a train...yumlike, blood, loads of blood and stuff... We're all over the papers, CCTV...

RUBE: Jesus.

TRAIN: ...I don't want it to mess stuff up, yeah?...yumlike magic Lex, she's going to colour me...

RUBE: When did it happen? Why didn't you tell me?

TRAIN: ...don't matter, just let me know if you see her...
(*Pause.*) Rube...
(*Beat.*)

RUBE: Yeah. I will. (*He hangs up.*) So, where were we?

LEX: I was just about to go.
(*She heads to the door, he cuts her off.*)

RUBE: Why didn't you tell me about that boy you assaulted?
(*Beat.*)

LEX: What boy?

RUBE: The one you attacked on a train. Sounds like you've had a good week; the boy, Trainers. Any other calamities you haven't mentioned?

LEX: Come again?

RUBE: What other fuck ups don't I know about?

LEX: Fuck ups? Why would I be involved / in any fuck ups...?

RUBE: Last night I helped you. You were upset. I took the time.
(*Silence.*)
Is he dead?
(*Pause.*)

LEX: I don't know.

RUBE: *Jesus...* Have you bothered to find out?

LEX: I'm hardly going to start ringing up.

RUBE: Well I would, I'd ring.

LEX: Yeah, I know you would. It's fuck all to do with you anyway.

RUBE: Of course it's to do with me...

LEX: No it isn't, it's between me and that boy. He'll get over it. You always do...

RUBE: Don't you understand how serious this is?

LEX: *Yeah.* Do you? Anyway, they've got to catch me first.

RUBE: Well they'll catch you alright, because I'll ring the police myself.

LEX: *You do that and I'll break your fucking neck.*

RUBE: So let me help you.

(*It clicks.*)

LEX: Right, I get it.

RUBE: You don't need to 'get' anything.

LEX: Help me do what exactly?

RUBE: I don't know... You're not stupid, you can do things...

LEX: Fuck's sake... Did Shell really...? I can't believe my sister's just going to fucking... What did you tell her?

RUBE: That my name's Rube.

LEX: Why did you say you worked for social services?

RUBE: Is that what I said?

LEX: I heard you. I was in the bathroom.

RUBE: Well, I sort of do.

LEX: Yeah, but you either do, or you don't, you know what I'm saying? You said you work down a youth centre.

RUBE: I do.

LEX: Well that's not social services is it?

(*Pause. No answer.*)

RUBE: Your sister dug out some clothes, do you want to change?

(*He chucks a bag to LEX.*)

I did a big shop at Safeways, so we've got loads of grub. (*Beat.*) We can just, take our time.

(*She stares at him, controlling her anger. Starts to laugh.*)

It's not funny.

LEX: Yes it is.

RUBE: No it isn't.

LEX: No you're right it, fucking isn't.

(*She heads for the door. He blocks her way.*)

Get out my way.

RUBE: Don't go.

LEX: Move.

RUBE: Sorry. Lex... I'm sorry, alright? I'm just trying to say, what I was trying to say... You need to think...before you go back out that door... Lex, listen to me, before you walk back out that door and *sink*, yeah? Before you walk back out that door and fulfil your 'social fucking prophesy'...

LEX: My what?!!

RUBE: ...you need to stop for a bit, say to yourself: 'I'm going to think about all this.'

LEX: Yeah? Think what...?...Don't worry. I got it. You want me to be a good little family girl, yeah? / Good little wifey?

RUBE: You tell me.

LEX: Yeah, cos I heard it all before. Maybe even a job. So what you going to offer me, hundred, hundred and fifty a week? Get me wearing a smart knee length skirt, nice pair of heels, then no one gets worried what I might do with this, yeah? (*She shows him her fist. Pause.*) No one controls me. I'm uncontrollable.

(*Silence.*

Music plays.)

15

SHELLEY's kitchen. She has the tracksuit top LEX left behind, she smells its smell, folds it. She takes up the fags she carries, starts to count them under her breath.

16

RUBE's flat as before. RUBE stares at LEX, wipes his lip with a handkerchief. Silence, until...

LEX: What time is it?

(*No answer. Long silence.*)

S'hot in here.

(*No answer. Still RUBE watches her.*)

You make it all sound so easy, you know what I'm

saying?

RUBE: It's not easy.

LEX: No. Cos there's people out there don't like me, yeah? /
    I seen it, when I'm standing in the courts...

RUBE: No... Yeah?

LEX: Yeah. When I got those magistrates and stuff...

RUBE: Right.

LEX: Yeah. They're peering down at me. Deep down they're
    going to feel better giving me the... By locking me up...
    I know it, they know it.

RUBE: So you'd rather be in prison?

LEX: What you on about? People like you, you bollock on
    how I can't be like I am, and all the time you don't have
    to wake up being me, yeah?... (*Short pause.*) That's all
    I'm saying. Open the door now, please.

RUBE: So use the thing.

LEX: Did you *listen* to what I just said?

RUBE: That whoosh thing you talked about last night...
    start it up. Choose it how you want it. It's the same thing
    everyone struggles with every day of their lives. That
    whoosh thing doesn't make you different Lex, it makes
    you the *same.*
    (*Silence.*)

LEX: What you getting out of all this?

RUBE: Me?

LEX: Yeah. This...acting like some fucking preachy clingon
    ...like some... (*Beat.*) Why should you care about me?
    This time last week you didn't even know me.

RUBE: I know I didn't.

LEX: So what's the situation?

RUBE: There isn't one.

LEX: You don't think so?

RUBE: What I'm saying, every word, every sentence, it
    makes sense.

LEX: Yeah, but it's your sense, you're like everyone else I
    ever met...like you're fucking...like you want to take me
    apart, you know what I'm saying? Take me apart and
    make me fit some fucking scheme...

RUBE: Yeah, because what happens otherwise?

(*No answer.*)

Eh?

(*No answer.*)

Eh?

LEX: I don't know.

(*Beat.*)

RUBE: If you don't fit the scheme, you end up so far out of your depth you can't ever get back to the shoreline.

LEX: What fucking shoreline?

RUBE: The *shoreline*? It's...it's wherever you want it to be, it's in your head, it's just...it's... I do this, I do that. People say, 'Let Rube do it, he's reliable.' The routine: of getting up, of being respected.

LEX: That's what you get off on is it?

RUBE: It's what I *fight* for, yeah. I know you think I don't know, but there was times I didn't think I could get back. I was drowning...in the violence, the hate I had, the fucking... I've lived the pain you've got now Lex, but I shook it off.

LEX: Why, what happened to you?

(*No answer. Silence.*)

RUBE: It doesn't matter about me / it's you I'm focusing on.

LEX: See, that's not fair! no one ever tells me the things I want to know...

RUBE: Coming out of the water, at the shoreline...all of a sudden it's like you're free. You don't understand what I'm trying to do because I can't really understand it myself, I just now that I'm afraid of...myself. And when I saw you, when I first walked into your flat, I walked, into your flat, I just, I walked, I came, in, and I saw. You. And it was like instinct, madness, putting myself next to someone like you, but instinct. I thought maybe I should care for you... Nothing else.

(*Silence. RUBE looks down at the knife, turns away, puts it down. As he does, LEX heads for the door again. RUBE turns, blocks her path.*)

No. Where you going?

LEX: Home.

RUBE: The door's locked.

(*Beat.*)

LEX: What?

RUBE: It's locked.

LEX: *So fucking open it!*

RUBE: *Sit down.*

(*LEX goes wild suddenly, like a button has been pushed.*)

LEX: *Open the door, open the fucking door…!!!!*

RUBE: Sit down.

LEX: *You want me to put my hand through that fucking window…!!?*

RUBE: *You come into my house then you show some respect…*

LEX: *Don't want to be here…you're the one making me stay here…*

RUBE: *Sit down…*

(*In a flash, RUEBEN takes LEX by the throat, swift, surprising her. And he holds her, squeezing. Until…*)

LEX: (*Gasping.*) …bastard…

(*They are nose to nose, and then he stops, releases her. Now LEX is crying, desperate. RUBE waits, watches.*)

RUBE: Lex.

LEX: Keep away from me…

RUBE: I went too far… I'm sorry… I…

(*A change has come over LEX, like in the very first scene on the train, like when she beat up TRAINERS. LEX grabs RUBE, digging her nails into his eyes. She pulls him to the table and smashes his face on it, one, two, three, four, five times. He drops to the floor. LEX stands above him, and now the words come again, first in a blurt, and then growing steadier, more rhythmic.*)

LEX: …magic out better out let it out in doesn't make it out it's bad magic and out lets it come out lets it come in doesn't make it out can't keep out in it's you it's magic Lex so out out let it out out…

(*LEX takes the hot tea pot and pours it over him. RUBE cries out, is half conscious with the pain, groaning. As LEX kneels*

and rubs the tea leaves into his face, a mobile rings.
TRAINERS and SHELLEY speak.)

SHELL: Hello?... Hello?

TRAIN: ...yumlike, what you doing Shell...?

SHELL: Lex left her phone here... She's at Rueben's house...

TRAIN: ...yumlike, but I rang him... He said she wasn't there... Shell...? Shell...?

(*Back in RUBE's flat, LEX opens the Angel Delight mix, sprinkles it on RUBE, sprinkles black pepper, digs in the bin and pulls out carrot scrapings, potato peelings.*)

LEX: ...it's in it's Lex it's you it's Lex so out out let it out out it's in it's Lex it's you it's Lex so out out let it out out it's in it's Lex it's you it's Lex so out out let it out out it's in it's Lex it's you it's Lex so out out let it out out it's in it's Lex it's you it's Lex so out out let it out out

(*Continuing her words underneath, LEX takes the knife and lines the blade against RUEBEN's fingers on one hand. She draws the blade over them, and through his unconsciousness, RUBE screams out in agony.*

LEX drops the knife. Exhausted by her attack, she slumps next to the bloodied and disgusting looking RUEBEN. In LEX's flat, LORNA has entered, ADDY sees her.)

ADDY: Where you been?

(*Silence.*)

LORNA: You alright?...you got holes in your eyes, you've got a face like a ghost.

ADDY: What?

LORNA: I said, you alright?...you got holes in your eyes, you've got a face like a ghost.

(*Silence.*)

I was waiting under the shelter...I could see the whole of the station. Two hours, three... (*Pause.*) Sorry. (*Beat.*) I need my bed for a bit, yeah?

ADDY: I told you not to ring them.

(*Beat.*)

LORNA: Yeah.

(*ADDY sits, LORNA crawls into him, sitting at his feet, her head in his lap. They hold each other. At RUEBEN's house, TRAINERS, and then SHELLEY, arrive at the front door. Banging on it.*)

TRAIN: Rueben.!!... I need to see you... / Rueben...

SHELL: Did you speak to her? Lex, open the door, yeah?

TRAIN: I need to see Lex...

SHELL: *Lex, open the fucking door, yeah?*

TRAIN: *Rueben...!!*

(*Inside, LEX searches for the keys to the front door. She digs them out of RUEBEN's pocket and opens the door.*)

SHELL: (*To LEX.*) What's happened?

(*SHELLEY pushes past her, sees RUEBEN.*)

Jesus...

LEX: I gone further Shell...

(*SHELLEY goes to RUEBEN.*)

SHELL: Trainers, get an ambulance.

(*TRAINERS doesn't move, just stares at RUEBEN.*)

Trainers, get a fucking ambulance...

(*SHELLEY shoves her towards the door. TRAINERS stops outside, calling by mobile. SHELLEY looks again at the mess LEX has made of RUEBEN.*)

Jesus...

(*LEX goes for the door, SHELLEY grabs her.*)

Where'd you think *you're* going...? You're fucking staying, come here...

(*She pushes LEX back down.*)

Think you're walking out...? Doing your usual...

(*RUEBEN groans, she goes to him.*)

Alright mate, ssssh, someone's coming.

LEX: He's not dead.

SHELL: That makes it alright does it...? What the *fuck* were you doing?

LEX: *Don't have a go at me, you're the one left me alone / with a fucking nutter.*

SHELL: I didn't leave you... I thought he was, he said he could help you... Fuck.

(*LEX moves to go again.*)

I said you're *staying*. You're going to listen.

LEX: I don't want to listen.

SHELL: Yes you do... All the years I've stood watching
you... Look at him, don't you think you've got to the
end of something, yeah?... It's not written down
somewhere, like you've got to keep going from one fuck
up to the other...like you can take the easy ride...

LEX: I'm not going to no fucking police station.

SHELL: I'll support you... There's nothing says you can't
ever just wipe the slate clean and just...do you know
what I'm saying? Like me, like Carl...like the kids, look
at us...every day I scream...at Carl, at the kids, cos
there's things it's our right to have, as a family.
Happiness...and, it's just...
(*Pause.*)

LEX: Dad never made you bad.

SHELL: What? (*Pause.*) No. But it was me that found him in
the garage... It was me had to run to mum, yeah...?
Fuck. It's only like an example I'm giving you: that I
don't ever give up, that sometimes me, Carl, the kids, we
get so fucking happy and stuff, and it's so brilliant, and I
don't ever want you to...
(*RUEBEN groans again.*)
Alright mate...ssshh.
(*She strokes his head. LEX sits. SHELLEY sits also. Waits.*)
Where is it?...

LEX: What?

SHELL: Your half... I know you carry it...
(*She puts her own half of the photo on the table. LEX stares
at it, digs her own half from her pocket. SHELLEY places
them side by side.*)
That's you, that's me. That's mum, that's dad.
(*Pause.*)

LEX: S'faded...
(*Beat.*)

SHELL: Join em up...
(*LEX stares at the two halves of the photo. In LEX's flat,
LORNA turns to ADDY.*)

ADDY: (*To LORNA.*) I love you.

(*They stand, ADDY turns the lights on, off, on, off, on, off, on, off. He and LORNA leave.*
In RUBE's flat, LEX stands, stares down at the photos, looks at SHELLEY, and goes. At the door, she meets with TRAINERS.)

TRAIN: ...yumlike...

(*LEX runs her hands over TRAINERS' face, over the bruises she inflicted.*)

LEX: Later Trainers...

(*She goes. SHELLEY grabs the two halves of the photo.*)

SHELL: Stay with him Trainers...

(*SHELLEY follows LEX, and TRAINERS is left alone. Music plays. As it does, TRAINERS moves slowly towards the injured figure of RUEBEN. She kneels at his side, pulling him into her, holding his head, whispering.*)

TRAIN: ...good come good come come come good come good come come come. Good. Come...good come good come come come good come good come come come. Good. Come...good come good come come come good come good come come come. Good. Come...

(*Until end.*)

KID

Characters

LEE
twenty-four

ZOE
twenty-five, seven months pregnant

K
twenty-five

BRADLEY
thirteen

It is the summer. August. Hot.

Kid was first produced by Theatre Absolute, in co-production with the Belgrade Theatre, Coventry. It was previewed on 15 July 2003, at the Belgrade 'Theatre Within a Theatre'. The play subsequently transferred to the Edinburgh Fringe Festival, premiering at the Pleasance Cavern. The cast was as follows:

LEE, Paul Simpson

ZOE, Samantha Power

K, Richard Oldham

BRADLEY, Rebekah Manning

Director, Mark Babych

Set design, Dominie Hooper

Lighting design, Simon Kemp

Soundscape, Andy Garbi

Stage Manager, Lizzie Wiggs

Technician, Claire Dickinson

Press Agent, Martin Shippen

Producer, Julia Negus

1. The symbol / indicates an interruption point.

2. Lines in italics are for emphasis, not necessarily volume.

1

K and LEE in a bar, the night of LEE's birthday, the day K just got out of jail.

K: ...it's one of my stories, you like my fucking stories....
Motor pulls up. Sleek, fat, silver gut four wheel drive,
and the window goes down... (*He does the motorised
window noise.*) Yeah? Window goes down and this
cockney wide boy voice, 'Alright mate, is this the way to
the 'ospital... (*LEE is laughing.*) Fuck's sake it's Rio
Ferdinand doing some Man U charity trip. So I'm rip,
swift as a fart at a cauliflower party, into the car and I'm
like... Me and The Ferdinand. S'like he is on *Match of the
Day*, lips going sideways, smiling like suddenly he's got
nervous, and I'm all, yeah you *better* get nervous
Ferdinand, where's the wallet, where's the cash, how
come you've got all this, give me some of what you've
got, cunt. Rio's had it man, didn't he think before he
stopped to ask, way I'm feeling, way that road I been
walking is all long and endless, didn't he think about
choosing someone else? You seen inside those Chrysler
S300's, all dials and luxury seats, his cockney crawl
'Listen mate' and I'm fist clenched, I'm feeling it, 'Listen
mate, you better get out...' I want him to say it, 'Do you
know who I am?' I want him to ask me, ask. Go on, ask
me if I know who you are. Cos I'm me, and Ferdinand
you're fucked, today you're going to pay... Bastard
pushes me in the chest, I'm backwards out the door
sumersault into the gutter, puddles, and my fist full of
hate. Rio's at the door, gas down and he burns the tyres.
There's me legging it after him high like a kite and the
Feds come cruising round the next corner. I'm on the
kerb doing up my laces, stop, think, don't breathe. Plod
one gets out, 'Alright K?', they know me, doesn't
everyone know me? Plod 2, I spit at him, and go!!... K's
running! Can't keep the K down! (*Beat. To someone behind
him.*) You laughing. What's so funny?

(*To LEE.*) You pissed, yeah? I'll get us another. We're
going to have a great night.
(*Music plays.*)

2

The present.

*In the yard of his house, LEE lies drunk. To the side is a cool box full
of beer. In one area, is a thin strip of a flower bed.*

Silence.

*LEE is alone, until BRADLEY and ZOE come out of the house with
a bowl of ice cubes, and ZOE starts to undo LEE's trousers. She
manoeveures LEE's jockey's down. LEE stirs. The girls stop. ZOE
scoops up some ice. She prizes LEE's buttocks apart. By now she and
BRADLEY are in stitches, it's generally a messy affair and the shock
of the ice sends LEE jumping before ZOE can make any real
'impression.'*

LEE: What you doing!!!?
    (*LEE falls over, tripped up by his own trousers.*)
    What the fuck's going on?!!
BRADLEY: We're shoving ice up your arse.
LEE: *What?*
ZOE: Ice. I read about it. You were out cold, you haven't
    moved all afternoon.
BRAD: Thought you might be dying bro. / Alcoholic
    poisoning.
LEE: Yeah, right.
BRADLEY: Your wife was worried.
LEE: Not my wife.
ZOE: I thought you might be choking.
LEE: So you shove fucking ice cubes up my ring, yeah?!
BRADLEY: Got a whole bowl full.
    (*ZOE and BRADLEY burst out laughing again.*)
LEE: Very funny. (*To BRADLEY.*) You look at my tackle? (*To
    ZOE.*) I only had a few cans.
ZOE: The fridge is empty.

BRADLEY: Couldn't see nothing.

LEE: Right, and so suddenly I'm dying, drowning in my own sick? (*LEE inspects his shirt.*) No spew I notice.

BRADLEY: No spew bro.

(*BRADLEY scoops some ice out of the bowl.*)

(*To LEE.*) You thirsty?

ZOE: Don't touch that, it's been up his.../...!!

LEE: Alright, alright, we get the picture.

(*BRADLEY carries the bowl back into the house.*
Silence.)

ZOE: I was looking after you.

LEE: Well fuck off, don't do it again. I was having a kip. (*Rubbing his arse.*) Where'd you learn about stuff like that anyways?

ZOE: *Q* mag.

LEE: You don't read that shite.

ZOE: Don't you?

LEE: Do I look it?

(*BRADLEY's mobile rings as she comes back out.*)

BRADLEY: (*Mobile.*) Yo?

ZOE: How'd you know it's shite then?

LEE: Cos it is. *Q Magazine.* You know what I'm saying?

ZOE: There was a photo of the Charlatans on the front.

BRADLEY: (*Mobile.*) Come round to the back gate.

LEE: Since when do you know about the Charlatans?

ZOE: Why wouldn't I?

LEE: Because you're all, Ibiza. *Now That's What I Call Music – 152.*

BRADLEY: (*Into phone.*) Sweet, see you.

LEE: Yeah.

(*BRADLEY gives LEE the thumbs up.*)

Sorted?

BRADLEY: Deffo.

ZOE: What is?

LEE: Bingo. (*Beat.*) So, Ice Up The Arse, what's the situ?

ZOE: *What* is? Who was on the phone? Is that one of your 'mates' coming over?

(*No answer.*)

ZOE: Pathetic.

LEE: What?

ZOE: We've only been here two days and already you're...
  (*She points at her belly.*) *You want this do you?*

LEE: What?
  (*Silence. They face each other.*)

LEE: Kid's got nothing to do with it.

ZOE: No?
  (*Silence. He goes to the cool box; it's empty.*)

LEE: Caught the sun there Brad. Excuse me while I get
  some refreshments. Any requests? Zo? (*No answer.*)
  Bradley? Cold drink from the frigidaire?

BRADLEY: Beer bro, cheers.

LEE: Coke.

BRADLEY: Bastard.
  (*LEE goes inside. Pause. BRADLEY moves across to ZOE,
  rests her hand on her sister's belly.*)
  Not long.

ZOE: No.

BRADLEY: I'm going to buy it stuff.

ZOE: Are you?
  (*Beat.*)

BRADLEY: Nah.

ZOE: You'll be its Aunty.

BRADLEY: Uncle, bro.

ZOE: Bradley.

BRADLEY: *What?...* B, call me B bro.

ZOE: What do you think of the new house?

BRADLEY: Alright.

ZOE: Do you like your room?

BRADLEY: Not mine is it?

ZOE: Kind of.

BRADLEY: Only while I'm here.

ZOE: Yeah.

BRADLEY: Liked the last one better.

ZOE: Did you?

BRADLEY: We going into town, or what?

ZOE: I don't know. We need to hang around for a bit. K's been in touch, said he's coming to see us.

BRADLEY: Here?

ZOE: Yeah. I need to rest anyway.

BRADLEY: That's cos of FuckBucket. Next time you move house, let him do it all, shouldn't be lifting boxes in your state. (*Of LEE.*) Lazy twat.

(*Silence.*)

ZOE: Bradley, don't you think it's time you went moved home?

BRADLEY: Like being with you.

ZOE: I know you do, but this is me and Lee.

BRADLEY: Yeah. So you live with mum and dad then. You get the frown, and I'll stay here.

ZOE: No thanks.

BRADLEY: Right. So. Cos I get the frown. I'm sitting on the bog for an hour, two; I been sitting on the bog to keep away from them frowning.

ZOE: It's not just them, it's you as well.

BRADLEY: What've *I* done?

ZOE: They're pissed off arguing with you all the time.

BRADLEY: Tough bro.

ZOE: Well then they won't want you back, will they?

BRADLEY: Yo. So?

ZOE: So what?

BRADLEY: So I'll stay with you.

ZOE: No... *Yeah*, but I didn't mean.../ Go and stay with Kels, why don't you stay with Kelly for a bit?

BRADLEY: Yeah. (*Beat.*) No chance, not staying with *her*. Stuck up bitch.

ZOE: Bradley.

BRADLEY: B.

ZOE: *I'm just saying:* you can't stay forever.

(*Pause.*)

How about you stop acting so smart all the time?

BRADLEY: I am smart. I'm the MC B. I'll move on when I've got my crew operating, how about that bro?

ZOE: Hardly.

BRADLEY: Yeah, got some contacts down the Black House.

ZOE: Not this again.

BRADLEY: Black House is *fine*. No one stops the Black House. Me and my crew operating, and we'll be like, Raaaaa! Gun down someone's throat, 'Give us your money...!'

ZOE: *Bradley.*

(*Silence.*)

Take your hat off.

BRADLEY: Nah.

ZOE: Come on, let me see you, you're gorgeous.

(*She grabs BRADLEY and they tickle each other until ZOE pulls BRADLEY's cap off, and her hair cascades down. ZOE takes it in her hands, smelling its aroma.*
LEE comes out into the yard.)

LEE: (*To ZOE.*) What time shall I start the barbie?

(*ZOE lets BRADLEY's hair drop from her hands, and heads into the house.*)

What did I say? (*She pushes past him. To BRADLEY.*) Where'd you tell those lads to come?

BRADLEY: Back gate.

(*He chucks BRADLEY some sun cream.*)

LEE: Put this on for us.

BRADLEY: Uh uh.

LEE: Come on, I'll burn up.

(*She squirts the cream out, rubs it half heartedly onto LEE's back.*)

LEE: That's why she's done a moody. Yeah? Like, the cops come, you know what I'm saying? And they do us cos we've got a load of knock off.

BRADLEY: Wounded.

LEE: True though. She gets dead worked up, like I'm still on the crime.

BRADLEY: I can see why bro.

LEE: Yeah, but I'm not though am I? Not really I'm not. Rub it in deep.

BRADLEY: Stinks. Zo says K's coming.

(*Beat.*)

LEE: Yeah.

BRADLEY: I'm going to do my rap for him.

LEE: Don't piss him off.

BRADLEY: Haven't seen him for ages.

LEE: A year.

BRADLEY: Yeah? So where's he been?

LEE: Good fucking question. Are you rubbing that in?

(*A car horn sounds. LEE and BRADLEY look to the street. Beat.*)

Sort it then.

(*BRADLEY chucks the cream back to LEE, goes into the entry and out to the street. LEE's mobile rings. During the phone call, BRADLEY brings various boxes of knock off into the yard.*)

Hello?....Who? Yeah, sorry, yeah that's me. (*He listens.*) Right. Why? Because I just want to know why I didn't get it, that's all. (*He listens.*) Right. Yeah, no, I mean if that's what you've decided. So you got anything else? I was thinking, you got any warehouse jobs, any fork lift truck stuff?...No, but I'm a quick learner. (*He listens.*) Yeah. Right.

(*LEE hangs up, and BRADLEY staggers through with the final box of knock off.*)

Get us a beer.

BRADLEY: What am I, your fucking slave?

(*BRADLEY puts the box down, goes to the cool box and gives LEE a can of beer. She opens one for herself.*)

LEE: (*Taking the can from her.*) Sorry, can't let you drink that.

BRADLEY: What?

LEE: You're in our / care, you know what I'm saying?

BRADLEY: Get lost.

LEE: I'm the daddy round here. *Stop fucking crying.*

BRADLEY: I'm not.

(*She turns away, wipes her eyes.*
Long silence.)

LEE: Give us a hand with this.

(*LEE gets out a line of fairy lights.*)

Bradders.

(*He opens another can of beer.*)

Can you take a joke, or what?

(*He hands her the can.*)

Fuck's sake.

BRADLEY: Ta.

LEE: Decorating the yard for Zo.

BRADLEY: Is this you being Mr Sensitive?

LEE: When am I never?…Stretch them over that way…

(*BRADLEY takes the lights across the width of the yard.*)

Tight, you fucking…

BRADLEY: I can't reach.

LEE: Stand on your tiptoes……

(*LEE secures the last section so that the lights, a pathetic chain of about ten, are now looped across the yard. They step back, admire their handiwork.*)

I can be very sensitive as it goes.

BRADLEY: (*Sarcastic. Indicating the box of knock off.*) Funny way of showing it, some poor granny's just had her tele robbed, scary men you just paid to break inside her house bro.

LEE: Yeah, but that's not my problem though is it? You snooze, you lose, you know what I'm saying?

(*He flops back down on the sunlounger.*)

BRADLEY: (*Nodding to the box of knock off.*) When do I get my split?

LEE: Soon.

(*Silence.*)

BRADLEY: So what time's K coming?

LEE: Don't know. Soon. Next question. (*Beat.*) I've got one actually: Where'd you get your black eye?

BRADLEY: Lad in year ten, started on me cos he said I was a girl.

LEE: Yeah? (*Beat.*) Bradley, you *are* a fucking girl.

BRADLEY: No bro. Boy. Girl by voice.

LEE: Right. *And* by tit.

BRADLEY: No.

LEE: *Yeah.* From where I'm sitting. By tit, by bush, by fanny, seen you fiddling, seen the 'Light Flow' in the bathroom.

BRADLEY: Zo's.

LEE: Get out, she's preggie. No periods when you're pregnant.

BRADLEY: Says who?

LEE: Er...Government? Who do you think you dozy cow?

BRADLEY: Girl by voice. Nothing else.

LEE: Right. So it's the old sex change then is it? (*Calling.*) *Zo, do they do sex / changes for 13 year olds?!*

BRADLEY: You wouldn't get lippy with me then. Men sort stuff. Control the order. Like The Man said.

LEE: Who's the man?

BRADLEY: The Man. Runs the Black House.

LEE: Thought me and Zoe warned you about going down there.

BRADLEY: No / bro.

LEE: *Yes* bro.

BRADLEY: They're like a family, do anything for you.

LEE: Like what exactly? Bradley, you keep going down that fucking Black House, and you'll go straight to the jail, or you'll end up dead, you know what I'm saying? (*Pause.*) We're trying to look after you.

(*BRADLEY blanks LEE, puts on her headphones and storms inside.*)

3

One year earlier.

Outside a prison. K stands before LEE. LEE holds a bag of lager. He gives it to K, who takes out a can and cracks one.

K: Can't keep a good man down.

LEE: Too right.

K: Good bye to that fucking jail, yeah? (*Shouting back to the prison.*) Goodbye to all you wankers who sail in it!

LEE: *K.*

K: What? They going to arrest me. Got to be bad first before they can arrest me. That's not hard for me and you though, yeah?

LEE: Yeah.

K: (*Shouting again.*) *Can't keep me, can't keep The K down!!* You not having one?

LEE: No.

K: Have one, have a fucking drink. I just got out didn't I?

LEE: Been drinking all day.

K: Yeah. It's your birthday. Where we going tonight then?

LEE: Dunno...I was going out with Zo and stuff.

K: Zo?

LEE: Yeah.

K: Your mate's been locked up for six months, and you want to spend the night with your bird?

LEE: What's wrong with that?

K: What's right with it? Tell her thanks for visiting by the way.

LEE: She couldn't make it.

K: Couldn't she fuck. She's never liked me. You don't have to protect her.

LEE: I'm not.

K: I'm only trying to look after you. So meet me by the tracks, yeah?

LEE: Eh?

K: Before we go out.

LEE: We're not fucking kids.

K: So what? I'll go and see my mum, then meet me by the tracks.

LEE: I told you.

(*K faces LEE.*)

K: I've looked forward to today. You here, meeting me at the gates.

LEE: I'm here aren't I?

(*K laughs.*)

K: Yeah. So we'll go down the tracks. Do a bit of Dead Man first. Missed doing Dead Man.

LEE: K...

K: And then we'll have a birthday drink. (*Beat.*) How's that sound?

(*K goes.*)

4

The present.

LEE is in the yard with BRADLEY.

LEE: Feels like it's getting hotter. Bradley?
BRADLEY: B.
LEE: What?
BRADLEY: The name's B bro.
LEE: Fucking bumble-B, yeah. Is it getting hotter, do-you-
    reckon?
BRADLEY: Yeah bro.
LEE: Zo, can we get one of those umbrella things? Going to
    be like this all month then we'll need some shelter.
    (*ZOE comes out of the house with a washing basket of baby
    clothes. She sees the box of knock off.*)
ZOE: Someone's been busy.
LEE: If I got my way we could live off shit like that.
ZOE: No we couldn't.
LEE: (*Points into the house.*) Yeah. All that in there, the three
    piece suite, the stereo, all that doesn't pay for itself, you
    know what I'm saying?
ZOE: That's why you need a job.
LEE: I know. Bingo. (*He holds up his mobile.*) Senior Shelf
    Stacker at Asda's, yeah?
ZOE: Did they ring? When do you start?
    (*No answer.*)
BRADLEY: Yo! Go bro, go bro.
ZOE: Bradley.
LEE: *Fuck off.*
ZOE: Whatever, we're not bringing our kid up / with a
    house full of someone else's stuff.
LEE: (*Daft voice.*) '…with a house full of someone else's
    gear… Stuff.' (*Beat.*) Happy enough to have it in the past
    though, yeah?
    (*LEE settles down on the sunlounger again, rolls a spliff.
    ZOE hangs out the baby gear.*)

LEE: Anyways, I been getting more honest lately. Nice to have a bit of praise now and then.

(*Pause.*)

BRADLEY: You're a very nice bro. How's that?

LEE: Cheers.

ZOE: What time is it?

LEE: Half six.

ZOE: He's not coming is he?

(*Pause.*)

LEE: I don't know.

(*BRADLEY goes to the plug for the fairy lights.*)

BRADLEY: Watch. (*No response.*) *Watch.*

(*BRADLEY puts the plug in.*)

Da, da!

ZOE: (*Unimpressed.*) Lovely. (*Pause.*) What we doing then?

LEE: Maybe he's delayed, like on the trains, and shit.

ZOE: We need to calm down.

(*LEE nods. Pause. He sees BRADLEY adjusting her bra strap.*)

LEE: Having a fiddle?

BRADLEY: Fuck off.

(*He laughs, heads back into the house, leaning over to tweak BRADLEY's tits as he goes. BRADLEY hits him, and they chase each other inside.*)

LEE: Nipple...nipple...

BRADLEY: Get off...

(*ZOE sits, half smiling at their laughter. A plane passes overhead. Then LEE and BRADLEY reappear, BRADLEY squealing as LEE attacks her with a water pistol, he slips and BRADLEY seizes the pistol, pinning him down and squirting water into his face.*)

LEE: That's enough...*I said that's enough you fucking...!!*

(*She chucks the pistol down and goes inside.*

Silence. LEE lies on his back, where he fell, watching the sky. Until...)

(*Nodding to the clothes horse.*) They look dead small them baby clothes.

(*ZOE holds one up.*)

ZOE: All washed and ready.

(*Silence.*)

(*To herself.*) Put that meat back in the fridge.

(*ZOE stands, and goes into the house.*)

5

One year earlier.

The deafening roar of a train as it powers through a tunnel. K and LEE face each other.

K: (*Calling.*) *Train's coming!!*

(*K leaps forward, grabbing LEE by the arms; they wrestle.*)

K: Dead man dead man dead man dead man.

Dead man dead man dead man dead man.

Dead man dead man dead man dead man.

LEE: Dead man dead man dead man dead man.

Dead man dead man dead man dead man.

Dead man dead man dead man dead man.

K: Dead man dead man dead man dead man.

Dead man dead man dead man dead man.

Dead man dead man dead man dead man.

LEE: Dead man dead man dead man dead man.

Dead man dead man dead man dead man.

Dead man dead man dead man dead man.

(*K is the stronger and the sound of the train gets closer.*)

Need to let me go now.

K: Dead man / dead man...

LEE: Let go now, fuck's sake...

K: How long you been the dead man, how many times you been the dead man?

LEE: More times than you.

K: How many times you been the dead man?

LEE: Always. Every time.

K: So make me the Dead Man.

LEE: Train's coming.

K: Make me the Dead Man. Fucking Birthday Boy...!!

LEE: Fuck off.

K: I want to be the dead man. I want to be the dead man.

LEE: Train's coming!!

K: No, you've got to make me, make me, see if you can make me.

LEE: I can't.

K: *I want to be the dead man.*

(*LEE tries to get him off and K grabs him, wrestling with him.*)

Fighting me...

LEE: Fucks sake...!!

K: Fighting me...yeah?...fighting...I'm going to be the dead man...

(*Still the train hurtles towards them.*)

I'm going to be the dead man.

LEE: *It's coming...K!!*

(*The train approaches, and they dive for cover as it roars past. As soon as it's gone, K is on his feet.*)

K: (*He thumps his chest.*) Living man, living man, couldn't take the living man!!

(*LEE is on his haunches, crying. K stops.*)

What?

(*LEE sobs.*)

LEE: What were you doing?... *We nearly fucking...*

K: It's a game.

LEE: When we were ten...(*He wipes his eyes.*). What's wrong with you?...What the fuck're trying to prove?

K: Me and you, that's what. Thought about you...(*Beat.*) In the jail.

LEE: Like what?

K: Like you're my family.

LEE: Not me, your mum.

K: No, *family.* You're all I've got. Like I'm you, and you're me. Like you're a bad influence on me. Like I'm a worse one on you. Like if this is all we'll ever be, then we'll be it together. Got my breath taken away every time I remembered, for when we were younger, when we were nicking cars, hotwiring, got edgy after I smelt the smell again, screeched rubber, shouts of the fuckers chasing us,

shouts of the angry world, 'you little bastards, bring my
car back...scum...'. chasing us up the road. I got these
nightmares, of me and you, hundreds like us, arrested,
packed off in trains, nightmares I got, of them hanging
me, shooting you, back of the head, cos we won't stop
being naughty. We say we're friends, and they pull us
apart, say we're not because we can't understand what
friends are. They send the train to huge fuck off plots of
land, it's a long way north, way north of cities, way north
of people, they have cells and fences to keep us in.
Thought about you, and about me, and Zo, and all the
other wankers I got to cross swords with, thought about
FiveFields, burning the shithole to the ground. All of it.
Made me tremble. Like I'm ready to explode. And I
knew, all the time, it was the jail, it was the cell, driving
me crazy. You know what it's like, trying to breathe in a
cell.

(*Beat.*)

LEE: Yeah.

(*Pause.*)

K: We going for that drink, or what?

6

The present. The next day.

*Alone in the yard, ZOE folds the baby clothes up. She stops, feels her
belly; where the baby is. She watches the sky. She makes a fist and
holds it above her belly, like she might punch it. She keeps it clenched,
breathes, will she? won't she? But stops as she becomes aware of
BRADLEY, who has come out and stood watching her.*

BRADLEY: What you doing....?

(*BRADLEY comes to her side.*)

ZOE: I was just...

(*Silence.*)

BRADLEY: You waiting for K again today?

(*No answer.*)

ZOE: Don't go saying nothing to Lee alright?

BRADLEY: What?

ZOE: About....

BRADLEY: It's his kid.

ZOE: Mine too.

BRADLEY: But your fist and that...I thought you were happy.

ZOE: I am.

BRADLEY: Doesn't / seem it.

ZOE: You wouldn't understand.

BRADLEY: Cos I'm stupid? I'm not, I see you lot. Mum, Dad, you, Lee. See you all bro.

ZOE: See what?

BRADLEY: Like I know what you're doing.

ZOE: Bradley, stop muttering, me and Lee aren't doing anything, we're just us, we're just having a kid.

BRADLEY: Yeah.

ZOE: So what then?

BRADLEY: You don't act natural.

(*Beat.*)

ZOE: Why don't we? *Why don't we?*

(*LEE comes back in from the street, calling from the entry.*)

LEE: Get that meat out the fridge Bradley, there's a good girl.

BRADLEY: *Boy.*

LEE: Girl.

(*BRADLEY goes inside. LEE has some barbecue tongs, newly bought. During the following, he busies himself with constructing a rough make of a barbecue; bricks, some coals, a shelf from the oven.*)

ZOE: Where you been? You said you were coming straight back.

LEE: Three Horseshoes, out on the main road. My old lady used to clean there, yeah? I used to go there as a kid, wait for her after school.

BRADLEY: (*From inside.*) 'Meat on Floor. Emergency. Meat on Floor. Emergency...'

(*BRADLEY comes out holding a burger between her fingers.*)

LEE: Be alright. Hide it under some salad.

BRADLEY: ShiteBucket.

LEE: Talking of which, I was thinking, it's alright round here, so best behaviour in the yard alright? No getting pissed and going naked in front of the neighbours. I'm talking about you Bradley, by the way, just cos you've started growing tits doesn't mean you need to go round showing them off to everyone!

BRADLEY: Not tits bro.

LEE: No?

ZOE: Leave her.

BRADLEY: Him.

LEE: *Her.*

(*BRADLEY does a King Fu kick towards LEE, just missing him.*)

BRADLEY: *Wah!!*

LEE: Watch it!!

BRADLEY: 'You're gonna cry/You're gonna die/
Cos I'm the Daddy/Cos I'm the boss/
Yeah, yeah, I see you hobblin'
Yeah, yeah, I see you grovellin'
(*LEE is laughing.*)

LEE: What's all that?

BRADLEY: Rapping. (*Beat.*) I'm a rapper innit.

LEE: You're a fucking kid, that's what you are.

ZOE: Bradley, ring mum. Work out when you can go home.

BRADLEY: No chance.

ZOE: *Just do it.*

(*BRADLEY doesn't move.*)

So I'll ring her myself.

BRADLEY: *Fuck's sake.*

(*Pause. There is a stand off between them. BRADLEY wilts, goes inside.*)

LEE: What's she done?

ZOE: Nothing, she hasn't done anything.

LEE: Doesn't look it.

(*ZOE waits, stares at LEE. Until…*)

ZOE: How long are we going to go on like this?

LEE: As long as it takes. / I don't know.

ZOE: When's he coming? *He said he was coming yesterday.*

LEE: I know. Look.../

ZOE: *Why's* he coming?

LEE: I don't know.

ZOE: (*Of BRADLEY.*) She knows.

LEE: Knows / what?

ZOE: *What do you think...?!*

LEE: What you said to her?

ZOE: Nothing. Something she said; we don't act natural.

LEE: Don't we?

ZOE: No, like we think we do, and like we don't, like it's showing.

LEE: Try not to panic.

ZOE: Some days I panic because I can't feel the kid, some days I panic because the sky keeps going dark.

LEE: What you panicking about the sky for?

ZOE: *Because I just am.* (*She looks to the sky.*) I'm thinking... 'Here it comes, now it's coming.'

LEE: Now 'what's' coming?

ZOE: Jesus always tells the truth.

LEE: Eh?

ZOE: What my mum and dad always said. I want to go to church.

LEE: When?

ZOE: Today.

LEE: *What?*

ZOE: Confess. / We'll be forgiven.

LEE: *No one's confessing nothing.* You don't say nothing to no one.

ZOE: I haven't.

LEE: You hadn't better.

ZOE: I haven't. Me, Kelly and Brad, we got brought up to be good kids.

LEE: Know you did.

(*Silence.*)

We're doing it for a mate.

ZOE: Yeah, and why are we? Cos it's the rules, FiveFields says we do it cos it's the rules. I hate the fucking rules.

LEE: *So fuck off then.*

ZOE: What?

LEE: Fuck off, I'll deal with it myself.

ZOE: No you won't. You can't... I can't.

(*Silence.*)

LEE: Everything'll be alright. Once the kid's here, wait and see. (*Pause.*) Anyways, you always knew the rep I've got, / you know what I'm saying?

ZOE: (*Exploding.*) *Rep?! What the hell are you talking about...? This isn't a game, why do you always carry on like / everything's a game?!*

LEE: I'm not.

(*BRADLEY comes back out, now dressed.*)

Not now Bradley, fuck off for a bit.

BRADLEY: Whoa bro.

ZOE: Don't take it out on him.

LEE: *Him.* What do you mean *him?*

ZOE: I mean her. *Her.*

LEE: Jesus, I give in! Go on, piss off / Bradley before I fucking...

ZOE: Keep your voice down.

BRADLEY: *B.*

LEE: Why the fuck should I!?!!

ZOE: Keep your voice down, the neighbours.

(*He kicks at the yard furniture, calls out to the neighbourhood.*)

LEE: Fuck them!! Come on, get your binnies out, yeah? Look at us, *look at us*...Look at those wankers just moved in. Get the Feds down, go on get the Feds down, fuck it all up...Come and get your free fucking bollocking off Zoe.

ZOE: Stop shouting...

LEE: ...get one of those looks the size of a footie pitch, one of those looks like you just farted and shat yourself all at the same time!! 'Who just farted', you know what I'm saying? Who just fucking... 'I'm the Queen Bee, I'm the star attraction, *I'm the only one pissed off round here!!*'

(*On the last line, the gate opens, and they stop, looking to K, who stands in the yard, his bag on his shoulder, a carrier bag in his hand.*
Pause.)

K: Alright? (*Beat.*) Alright Lee? Alright Zo?...(*Beat.*)
Bradley.
(*Beat.*)

BRADLEY: Wah! 'You is the K and you is here/ I is the
Brad and I is there/ Get the FBI telling...get the FBI
telling... Get the...get the, get....'
(*She runs out of ideas.*)
ShiteBucket.

K: Good try though.
(*Short pause.*)
(*To LEE.*) Good to see you.
(*He waits, and eventually LEE goes to him. They hug.*)

LEE: We gave up on you.

K: I said I was coming. (*Of the house, the yard.*) It looks
alright.

BRADLEY: Can't have pets.

LEE: Got one though. (*To BRADLEY.*) Go get Snoop Dog

K: Snoop Dog?

LEE: The cat.
(*BRADLEY goes inside.*)

K: I got yous this.
(*He holds out the carrier bag. LEE and ZOE stare at it.
ZOE takes it, puts it down by the side of the chair.*)

LEE: Cheers.

K: (*To LEE, of ZOE's baby.*) What's all that?
(*ZOE puts her hands over her bump.*)
Can't believe it.

ZOE: Why can't you?

K: Just...
(*Silence.*)

LEE: Get a bus up?

K: Cab.

LEE: I got some grub in, sausages, burgers. They're alright,
I don't think they've gone off. Want a beer?

K: Cheers.

(*LEE gets the cans. They chink them, drink.*)

LEE: How long you been back?

K: Two days. I'm off again tonight.

ZOE: So you were here yesterday?

(*BRADLEY comes back out.*)

BRADLEY: (*Sucking her finger.*) Cat Attack.

LEE: Give it a belt.

BRADLEY: What?

LEE: Needs to learn. Ask K, he taught a few in his time.

K: Not really.

LEE: What do you mean not really!? Fucking Chief Cat Exterminator over there...Walking back from school and things. Then he gets home and he changes into his combat gear, he's promoting himself, yeah?...He's fucking...he's Chief Cat, Dog, Fox, Squirrel, Bird, Hedgehog, Ant...he's whatever he could get his hands on fucking Exterminator, you know what I'm saying?

BRADLEY: Don't get foxes in cities bro.

LEE: Can do. We did. And one day, me, Zo and K there, using my old man's air gun, K's old man catches us, shot you in the leg yeah?

(*Beat.*)

K: Yeah.

(*Silence.*)

LEE: Dead surprised when you rang.

K: I bet you were. Your mum gave me your number. She was like, 'hello, hello...?'

LEE: What's she say?

K: Not much, never does anyway does she? (*Short Pause.*) You got e-mail?

LEE: Us? I get worked up doing that fucking Ceefax.

BRADLEY: (*To K.*) School has. ICT.

K: Right. You've grown nipper.

BRADLEY: Ages since I seen you.

K: Yeah, it's been a bit mad. I went away...(*He looks to LEE and ZOE.*) Ran into a bit of trouble.

ZOE: Is that what you call it?

(*No answer. Silence. Until...*)

K: Colder.

LEE: Than what? What's the temp today Zo? Zo's one of those weather watchers, keeps an eye on the weather. Must be 80, 82.

K: Since when?

LEE: Since about midday.

K: No, I mean since when did Zo watch the weather?

LEE: Always. She used to tell us on the way to school. 'Wear your coat today K; wear your wellies tomorrow Lee.'

K: (*To ZOE.*) Did you?

LEE: You forgot?

K: I just don't remember.

(*Silence.*)

BRADLEY: (*To K.*) I've got the back bedroom. Let me show you round. Let me do the voice.

LEE: *What fucking voice?*

BRADLEY: Tour guide bro...

(*BRADLEY moves inside, rapping as she speaks, her nose-pinched voice fading as she goes.*)

'On your left is the fireplace, and on the right is the door, it goes out into the kitchen...That's the tele bro...over there's the video control...'

(*BRADLEY goes inside and LEE calls after her.*)

LEE: *Shut the fuck up!!*

7

One year earlier.

LEE, ZOE, and K, in a pub. LEE and ZOE kiss, timing themselves on LEE's watch that he looks at over ZOE's shoulder. K looks on.

K: I bet that's your best pressie isn't it? (*They kiss.*) Bit of style at last. (*They still kiss.*) What a way to spend your birthday, snogging your 'girlfriend'. Cost me a fortune that did.

(*LEE breaks away from ZOE.*)

LEE: (*To K.*) I've said haven't I? It's sound. / Cheers.

ZOE: (*To LEE.*) How long?

LEE: Thirty-six seconds.

ZOE: (*To LEE.*) Come here!

(*She pulls him back, and they start kissing again. K's had enough, and pulls them apart.*)

ZOE: *K!*

K: (*To ZOE.*) Get us some more drinks.

ZOE: Like I'm your servant?

K: Yeah.

ZOE: We need to break our record.

(*ZOE and LEE laugh across K, reach for each other.*)

LEE: (*To ZOE.*) Come here...

ZOE: (*To LEE.*) Come and get me!

K: (*To ZOE.*) I just got out didn't I?

ZOE: (*To LEE.*) In a minute...stop him moaning.

(*Reluctantly, ZOE consents. She goes.*)

LEE: What's the matter with you?

K: Thought she wasn't coming.

LEE: She's alright.

(*He turns to follow ZOE. K takes his arm.*)

K: Don't ever mistake anything I do for jealousy; anything that happens, it isn't cos I hate you and Zo, alright?

LEE: Like what?

K: You're alright you and Zo, you've done okay mate. She'll get you married next. But don't come wanting to play Dead Man when she's got you married off, yeah? Kids, housey housey. Knows what she's after, knows what she wants Zo does.

(*LEE turns to go, K pulls him back again.*)

K: Don't ever get out the loop, yeah? She can't help you then... There's some things Zo can't help you with.

LEE: There is no fucking loop man, I do what I want, I come and go as I please.

K: You can still cum, she hasn't wilted all your powers then?!

LEE: It's alright, being in love, you should try it.

K: I don't need love.

LEE: Everyone needs love, no one wants to give it. I wake
up and there's no weight, I look at Zo and it helps me let
stuff pass. I'll let tonight pass; (*Pointing.*) the way that
guy there's looking at us, the way that wanker over
there's been eyeing up Zo, I'm letting it all pass, yeah?
Don't need to bruise some cunt cos it's going to make
me feel better. Even you, I'm forgiving you for trying to
fuck up my birthday all night. I'm just…

K: I'm not fucking it up, don't think I'm…Hey! (*He plants a
kiss on LEE's cheek.*) See me? I'm going to be drinking all
night. It's Lee's birthday, (*Calling to the club.*) *it's Lee's
fucking birthday!* No sleep, I don't sleep when I got
people around me, entertaining, I'll entertain you all
night, and then, see me? Morning time I'll be walking
the road to FiveFields, the length of it, yeah? Early
morning, like a road to hell, I'm going to be dizzy with
the length of it, rain's chucking, going to be needing
something, anything to keep the buzz going…you know
what I'm saying? You and Zo'll go home in an hour,
yeah? It's what you do, couples go home together, but
I'm staying up all night tonight drinking in honour of
YOU. I'll be on that road, morning, needing to keep the
buzz going, and I'll be thinking: what's happening up the
hills, maybe I'll go and murder a sheep or something,
and this fucking motor's going to pull up…

LEE: Zo's waiting.

K: It's one of my stories, you like my fucking stories….
Motor pulls up. Sleek, fat, silver gut four wheel drive,
and the window goes down… (*He does the motorised
window noise.*) Yeah?

8

The present.

*In the yard, ZOE sits with K's gift on her lap. LEE stands at the far
end of the yard. K watches ZOE as she opens the gift, reaches into the
box it's contained in, and takes out a small wind up toy. She winds*

it up and puts it on her open palm. The toy moves its arms, up and down, up and down. ZOE puts it on the floor.

Silence.

K: The house looks good. You've done okay.

ZOE: He's already been shouting, upset the neighbours. You'd think he'd have the sense to keep his head down.

K: What's the rent like?

(*She shrugs.*)

(*Of the baby.*) When's it due?

(*No answer. K looks to LEE. LEE shrugs, and goes back into the house. Silence, until...*)

ZOE: What are you doing here?

K: That's nice.

ZOE: *You want me to be nice?*

K: Tell me to go, and I'll leave.

(*Silence.*)

I was on a bus, about three months back... It was driving the coast road. I was delivering a parcel, doing odd jobs for people. I saw this girl, she turned round to look at me, she's in a seat further up the bus. She's like a backpacker. She looked like you.

(*Beat.*)

ZOE: Me?

K: And I'm suddenly... It's like I'm waking. I feel sick, and she keeps looking at me. My head starts aching. We stop at this roadside shack and I ask for water. I'm asking people for water, and they're looking at me. I'm white, sweating. I can see what they see: me, tiny, broken by a blast of something, the blast of remembering you, Lee, home.

(*ZOE sneers at him, goes to the flower bed. Plants some flowers.*)

K: That's when the headache comes, cos if I've thought of you, then you'll think of me, get inside my head, and then you'll see where I am, where I'm living. And then everyone else'll know. I can't stop my head aching, for days, weeks. I can't settle again. I want words I can understand, a conversation I can join in with. I left where

I was living, found myself back in the city. (*Pause.*) I didn't know what to think.

ZOE: You always know what to think

K: Not then I didn't. Now I do. Now I know why that girl affected me like she did.

ZOE: Why?

K: I hadn't known how alone I'd have to be.

ZOE: Worrying we might grass on you.

K: Sometimes.

ZOE: Before you came out of prison and fucked everything up, things were happening.

K: You think so?

(*LEE calls from inside.*)

LEE: Zo...??

ZOE: Lee seeing less of you for a start. I didn't want to chuck that.

K: So you would have, if it wasn't for him?

LEE: *Zoe...* Close your eyes...

BRADLEY: Raaaaaaaaaaa!! Drive by, drive by!!

(*BRADLEY and LEE emerge from the house. LEE has a baby's pushchair and BRADLEY is inside it. LEE pushes her at top speed around the yard.*)

Raaaaaaaaaaa!!

ZOE: Lee!

BRADLEY: Raaaaaaaa...

ZOE: Stop it.

BRADLEY: *Drive by. Drive by.*

ZOE: Lee!

BRADLEY: Drive by!!

ZOE: *Lee!!*

(*LEE stops. ZOE hauls BRADLEY from the pushchair.*)
It's bad luck.

LEE: Says who?

ZOE: It doesn't matter who, just get rid of it.

(*LEE tips BRADLEY out of the pushchair. The three of them watch each other, and BRADLEY saunters out into the entry, uneasy with all the tension.*)

9

One year earlier.

Music plays. In LEE and ZOE's kitchen. K stands with his arms out, breathing, gasping, and LEE and ZOE strip his clothes off.

K: *Quick...*
ZOE: I'm going as fast as I can.
K: *Is there anyone here?*
ZOE: Just get your clothes off... Lee... *Lee.* Get his shoes off.
  (*LEE gags, bent over.*)
K: Is there anyone here?
ZOE: No.
K: *If someone comes in they'll see us...*
ZOE: *Like who?!* There's no one here... Lift your leg, get this off your leg...
  (*She drags his jeans off. LEE grabs K by the throat.*)
LEE: *It was supposed to be a drink, it was just a birthday fucking drink!!*
K: Best jeans.
ZOE: *Not a joke.*
K: I wasn't.
  (*She inspects the jeans, throws them into the bag.*)
K: What about my pants?
ZOE: Get them off....Get them off and we'll dump everything.
  (*She waits as K strips off his pants. ZOE chucks K a pile of clean clothes.*)
  Get these on, and go.
K: Did anyone see us...
ZOE: Dunno.
K: What am I going to do... *??!!*
ZOE: Go to your mums.
LEE: *She* won't want to know.
  (*ZOE grabs at LEE.*)
ZOE: *You fucking promise me...*you fucking...don't EVER, you don't ever do *anything* again...no robbing, no

fucking about...you just...*This is it*....This is where it stops...
(*She stares at LEE.*)
Promise me.
(*He nods. ZOE looks to K, turns away, and leaves the room. Silence. LEE takes out a wad of notes.*)

LEE: Here. You'll need it...It's all I could get.

K: ...Where'd you get it?

LEE: Zo's old man, he gave her some cash. She's been saving up.

K: For what?

LEE: Stuff. Doesn't matter. Just take it.

K: Does she know you've got it?

LEE: *What do you think?* Just take it and get out the area, you know what I'm saying?
(*K rests his forehead on LEE's shoulder, looking at the cash in his hands.*)

K: He's alright Zo's old man... I always liked the way their house had that paving at the front; did her dad do that? I liked the way right, that you could walk through FiveFields, and his house was the best house on the estate. Her dad's pretty smart isn't he? And her mum. The way they've brought them up. Zo, Kelly, Bradley. They love them.
(*Silence.*)

LEE: Where are you going to go?
(*The lights fades.*)

10

The present.

K and BRADLEY in the yard.

BRADLEY: Do you want a game of Thumb Wars?

K: Not at the moment.

BRADLEY: You've grown your hair bro. Zo said you was coming back. Did you have a job?

K: Something like that. (*Beat.*) How's school?

BRADLEY: Shit...Missed you. Weird not having you around.

K: Weird not being around.

BRADLEY: You staying in England now?

K: No.

BRADLEY: *Yeah.*

K: Sorry. (*Beat.*) How come you're in the back bedroom?

BRADLEY: Been staying for a bit.

K: Why's that then?

BRADLEY: Stuff.

(*K looks back towards the house. As she talks, BRADLEY cuts out some holes in a cardboard box lid; she is making a 'Thumb Wars' arena.*)

K: What's it like living with Lee and Zo?

BRADLEY: Alright. They blank me, reckon I don't see it, but I see it fine bro. I've got plans anyway, going to move into the Black House. Do you know the Black House?

K: Yeah.

BRADLEY: Best house in FiveFields, on the Parade.

K: If you like that kind of thing.

BRADLEY: Don't you? Love those black metal sheets they've got over the windows. You know that special knock they've got? The Man opens the door and you go inside, and there's hardly any light, just a few bulbs. The Black House is the place. He lives there with some others, but you can stay for a bit if you're running, or you just need to chill. We drink and stuff, and sometimes The Man shows us the gun's he's got.

K: Guns?

BRADLEY: Knives, machetes, guns. I've seen them. He lies them out on a sheet; polishes them. We can touch, but we can't actually hold them, too heavy anyway. Heavy metal guns, and the machetes; take your fingers off. Inside the Black House, it's like your heart's beating. (*She touches the scuffs on his knuckles.*) Been fighting bro? I'll be the best fighter in my class soon. Got a black eye last week. Battered him though.

(*K ruffles her hair.*)

K: I was labouring. Stones, bricks.

(*BRADLEY puts her thumb up through one of the holes. K smiles. They play thumb wars.*)

BRADLEY: One two, three four...

K: I declare a thumb war...

BRADLEY: I declare a thumb war.

(*They play. BRADLEY wins.*)

One to me. I seen your brother in town on Monday.

K: Yeah? Did you speak to him?

BRADLEY: Zo did.

K: What's Craig say?

BRADLEY: Don't know. One, two, three four, I declare a thumb war.

K: ...two, three, four, I declare a thumb war.

(*They play.*)

BRADLEY: Two to me.

K: Bastard. Why aren't you living with your mum and dad?

BRADLEY: They're square bro, telling me how to behave all the time. One, two, three four, I declare a thumb war.

K: ...two, three, four, I declare a thumb war.

(*They play. K wins.*)

BRADLEY: One to you. Is that a Goatee?

K: Yeah.

BRADLEY: I like Goatees. Might grow a Goatee myself. We still playing?

K: In a minute.

BRADLEY: Where is it you been?

K: Do you know Central America?

BRADLEY: Mexico?

K: Near it.

BRADLEY: Did you go to the USA, the United States?

K: Passed through.

BRADLEY: FO.

K: What?

BRADLEY: Fuck Off.

(*LEE comes back out. He has the meat for the barbecue.*)

LEE: Chef's starting.

BRADLEY: Can I show you something?

K: If you want.

(*BRADLEY nips inside.*)

K: I thought you were blanking me.

LEE: She's been excited about you coming... She's started calling herself B. Zo told me. Anyone who talks to her they got to say B, not Bradley, 'B, can you get to bed?', 'B are you finished in the bog...?'

(*Long silence.*)

LEE: Where the fuck've you been?

(*BRADLEY returns, and the moment vanishes.*)

BRADLEY: (*To K.*) You seen this?

(*She puts a boxful of memorabilia on the floor. All of it American – badges, baseball caps, books, CDs.*)

(*She has a CD.*) Can't get this over here bro.

K: How come you've got it?

BRADLEY: Internet.

(*BRADLEY takes out a baseball cap.*)

Can't get this. Got it for fifteen dollars. You got any dollars on you now?

K: No.

BRADLEY: What's it like? Central America's not like proper America is it?

LEE: Central America?

K: Yeah. Guatemala.

(*LEE stares at K.*)

LEE: Fuck's sake.

K: (*To BRADLEY.*) It's different.

BRADLEY: How?

K: I don't know. You've got the sea for a start.

BRADLEY: America's got the sea.

K: Yeah, I know, but I reckon where I've been, it's like a real sea.

The sort of sea I used to think about when I was a kid.

BRADLEY: What else?

K: There's mountains.

BRADLEY: Big ones?

K: Huge. Mountains; and these big green trees. They roll down to the sea. In the water, you can see your hand. It's like a fish, the way it moves round you, pink, white, the colour of your blood. You pull it out, and you lick it cos the water's so fresh. On this tiny beach I found, there's no one there to see you, and so you just stroll around; you're naked.

(*BRADLEY laughs. During this next section, ZOE comes back out.*)

When I first got there, I was in the capital. I couldn't stand it, crappy hotels, the heat, too much noise. I headed towards the country. I didn't know where I was going to stay, but there was just this sun, warm. I talked to people I didn't know. I started cleaning shoes.

LEE: You were cleaning shoes?

K: Yeah. I go down, I get up. It's how I get by. And this guy I meet, he sells bits of fruit and vegetables outside his house, he gets a spare room cleaned up for me. Every day I go and collect the milk. He's got three goats.

BRADLEY: *Goats?*

K: It's a walk past this big chocolate coloured mountain I can see, way off. I've started to look at it, I've thought how it belongs to me. Night times, I end up working on a fishing boat, just bobbing in the harbour, cleaning the nets. I can't speak the language, but this old woman, she tells me a few words. I went to school until I was sixteen, yeah, I leave and I can hardly read and write, I spend ten months in this village and I've learnt a lifetime. (*Beat.*) Nearly killed me.

LEE: What did?

K: Being out there. There was a storm, from the mountains. I never heard anything like it.

BRADLEY: What's it sound like?

K: It's hard to describe. A whole day, rumbling, and then it rained, three days of rain, and then this flood sweeping through the village. The flood's rolling down that mountain I've been watching. I've called it The Nest cos of the birds I've seen swirling round the peak. But then

it's death mountain. I call it Death Mountain cos it's
pouring this mud and this water.

LEE: (*Laughing.*) Fucking 'Death Mountain'.

K: It's not a joke though, you know what I'm saying?

LEE: Sounds it.

K: Yeah. But the rain's not stopping, and I see these taxi
drivers, they always wait outside the post office, the
policeman, (*To ZOE.*) the craft stalls where I got that toy,
the kids crossing from the school, do you know what I
mean? They're all swept away.

LEE: Yeah?

K: Yeah. I'm like you, I can't believe it, and I'm watching it.
I grab onto a tree, and then I leg it down towards the
square cos I can hear people screaming, crying. I'm
running faster than the mud slide.

LEE: Bollocks.

K: Feels like it. There's houses down the main street,
cracking, like my leg when I was thirteen...
(*LEE laughs at this.*)
It's mad, yeah?...And I get to the square and there's
loads of people. Some of them I know, I've polished
their shoes, and they're splashing up and down, they're
drowning. I want to leg it again. It's too big for me. I
stare at them, they're reaching out. Like this...Like
this... (*Beat.*) I saw a kid floating on its back, getting
dragged under by the current. Suddenly I dived in and I
got it, then it flipped out of my hands. She went under. I
got her again, held her up, like this. I felt sick. I felt
myself going under, I got a mouthful of mud, water, two,
three; suddenly I couldn't stay up.

LEE: You're a good swimmer.

K: I know. I'm telling myself that. (*Silence.*) I'm a cunt Lee.
All my life, people hating the cunt in me. It's in my
head, and I don't want the kid to go under with me. I
don't want to die, not now. (*Silence.*) I grabbed her. I
pulled her up onto the bank. Held her.
(*Silence.*)
I've worked with them. I've helped them re-build.

ZOE: Why?

K: They asked me. They said: 'Will you stay? Will you help us?'

(*Long silence.*)

K: You should come back with me.

LEE: Sounds like a fucking disaster area.

K: No. They'll welcome you.

BRADLEY: What about me?

LEE: Probably get left in quarantine. They'll keep you at the airport and stuff, (*To K.*) don't they keep dogs and shit at the airport?

K: Yeah.

LEE: (*To BRAD.*) See. They'll have to get you checked for diseases before they can let you into their country.

K: I just reckon if you were out there, with me, it'd solve everything.

LEE: Me and Zo get dizzy going into town on the bus, wouldn't know what to do.

K: You'll do things you haven't thought of.

ZOE: (*To K.*) Don't you think it's wrong?

BRADLEY: (*To K.*) I'll come.

K: (*To ZOE.*) How?

ZOE: (*To K.*) Don't you have to earn it?

K: (*To ZOE.*) There's others get things they don't earn. Others all the time, getting things they don't earn.

LEE: (*To K.*) How long's the flight?

K: Twelve hours.

LEE: On a *plane?!* (*He cracks open another can.*) Send us a postcard, you know what I'm saying! Anyone for grub?

ZOE: *Not now.*

LEE: Barbie, yeah?

ZOE: *I said not now.* (*She looks back to K.*) We haven't finished talking.

LEE: We've got all afternoon.

ZOE: No, I want to carry on. (*To K.*) Not just about your 'backpacking' trip. I want to talk about real stuff.

BRADLEY: Like what?

(*Silence.*)

LEE: (*To BRADLEY.*) Clear off for a bit.

BRADLEY: Eh?

LEE: *Just fuck off will you?!*
  (*BRADLEY sighs, goes.*
  Silence.)

K: (*To ZOE.*) So?

ZOE: What do you / mean 'so'?

K: You said you wanted to keep talking.

ZOE: Yeah. (*Beat.*) Just to say that we've had enough. When you rang us, we talked about it, we said if you were coming to see us then we were going to put an end to everything, tell you we're not carrying on like this anymore.

K: Like what?

ZOE: Don't play games.
  (*Pause.*)

K: (*To LEE.*) You agreed with Zo did you? We're mates aren't we?

LEE: Course we are, but you're the one jumped ship.

K: Who jumped?

LEE: You.

K: No.

LEE: *Yeah...*What's all that shit about the...coming back, blabbering on about floods and shit. You think we care about a bunch of fucking... Why you acting like this? Minute you walked through that gate, way you're speaking, like you're fucking... Zo's right, we need to sort stuff out. *You fucked off, you left us.* I thought you'd go to Ireland, Scotland, not fucking *Guatemala.*

K: I didn't. I went to Florida first. I tried to ring.

ZOE: When? You could've kept trying, you could've written. We're still here, *we've been here.*

K: With each other.

LEE: You think that's easy? You just enjoyed time clear, you know what I'm saying? Some new country where no one knows you.

K: No one knows you either, you just moved in didn't you?

LEE: They do, they will. Other side of town, not the other
    side of the world…We *had* to move. We haven't stopped
    moving! This is the *sixth* house we've lived in this year.
    Some neighbour gets friendly with us, we move out
    again. Keep our heads down.
    (*LEE puts his head inside the house to be sure BRADLEY*
    isn't within ear shot. Steps out again.)
    You don't know how it's been. It's not safe. Feds've been
    back down FiveFields.

K: When?

LEE: All the time. It hasn't just gone away, yeah? They had
    you fingered right away.

K: I know.

LEE: Yeah. So we had to move. I'm the Invisible Man, you
    know what I'm saying? The last year, I can't claim dole,
    I'm applying for jobs with made up names, I don't even
    know if Zo should register me as the kid's dad. They
    trace me, they start getting to you, yeah?

K: Yeah. (*Pause.*) Thanks.

ZOE: *Don't thank him.*

LEE: Meanwhile, we're hemmed in, fucking ladyboy in the
    bedroom next to us.

ZOE: *Who?*

LEE: Bradley.

ZOE: Don't call her that.

LEE: Why not? She's a freakhead. And you, that whining
    fucking voice: 'Drop the crime, be honest, promise you
    won't ever be in trouble again.'

ZOE: Piss off.

LEE: *Ever.* Like that. You say it like that.

K: But she did. The last time the three of us were together,
    she made you promise.
    (*Beat.*)

LEE: Yeah. Well I'm breaking my back turning over that
    new leaf, you know what I'm saying?
    (*Beat.*)

K: I've succeeded.

ZOE: *What?* You murdered someone, or did you forget about that?

(*Long silence. K looks at ZOE, at LEE.*)

LEE: So why you back? I don't get it.

K: To see you two. My mum.

LEE: You said you were coming yesterday…

K: I was.

LEE: Where you staying?

K: B&B. In London. I got a train up this morning. I've got a false passport. When I go again, that's it.

LEE: Might never catch you.

K: Not with a record like mine.

LEE: How? You're a thief, you're a robber, you're like me, it's not like you go round beating people up every day of your life is it?

ZOE: Not every day, no.

K: You trying to be funny?

ZOE: *No, you're the one that's funny.* I mean, is this what you came all the way back for, to stand here in the sun and tell us stories, to take the piss out of us? (*Pause.*) What did you come all this way back for?

(*K stares at her. Swallows.*)

Yeah, well whatever it was, we've had enough of sitting around, covering up for you. (*She touches her bump.*) We've got stuff to get on with, in case you'd forgotten! So what are we going to do about it?

K: How do you mean?

ZOE: *Are you stupid, are you thick?!*

K: *Fuck off!*

(*LEE pulls K away.*)

LEE: Calm down.

(*LEE moves K to the back of the yard. ZOE sits, gets her breath. The mood settles.*
Long silence.)

K: (*To LEE.*) Do you want the kid?

LEE: Yeah. (*Silence.*) Don't know why, don't know why I feel like this. (*Pause.*) Zo says it'll be infected. Turn out the same. Do the same things…

ZOE: Not anymore.

LEE: What?

ZOE: I don't think that.

LEE: You said it. (*Pause.*) Three months after…We know what happened to us, but we don't talk about it, you know what I'm saying? We're sat in front of the telly and we're not watching. Just drinking. 'Phets, to get us out of it. We're tripping, lying in our pit, and no one's talking about it, what you did that night, what me and Zo both watched you do. And there's one night when I…my neck, my ears, tight, like I can't swallow, and I turn to Zo. I start kissing her. I grab her, pull her over and she pulls me back, grabs me by the throat, kisses me like I'm air. We shove and fucking…it's not love, we don't make it, (*To ZOE.*) do we? (*To K.*) You know what I'm saying? We jack it, we have it, and then we chuck it away. I ride her like she's meat, and she rides me back, staring down, mumbling shit at me, scratching my skin, no pill, no johnny, nothing, just the thought of a kid…being made out of someone dying. Makes me sick. I stand on the balcony, throw up, see the kids on the corner chucking bricks at the Paki shop, and I hear Zo in the bedroom… 'The kid'll be infected…' (*Silence.*) If I can give it something, you know what I'm saying?

K: You will.

(*Pause.*)

LEE: How?

(*Silence.*)

K: That old woman, in the village where I've been living, you'd like her, every day she taught me a bit of Spanish. She's not poor, she's rich. She's got a mansion at the end of the village, and she walks the harbour with her cat, it's on a lead. She taught me words and phrases that I wrote down, like they're all the words I'll ever need.

(*Silence.*)

I'm sick about missing the birth.

LEE: (*Hardly able to speak.*) You'll be in Honolulu.

K: Where?

LEE: Fucking, somewhere erotic.

(*Beat.*)

K: Exotic.

(*Beat.*)

LEE: That's what I said didn't I!!

(*LEE storms inside, passed by BRADLEY coming the other way, dressed up in even more rapper gear, carrying a CD player.*)

BRADLEY: What's up with FuckBucket?

(*No answer. BRADLEY puts her CD player down. Turns it on. She starts:*)

BRADLEY: It's de MC B in da' house. Yo. Yo...

Bum-bumbling waiting for the humbling,

Watching the heavyweight rumbling...

It's the fastest show on Earth, when Bradley...

ZOE: *Bradley...*

BRADLEY: Who's always hard and never sadly...

ZOE: Bradley! What you doing?

BRADLEY: Walks into the town, and makes the people frown... (*She stops.*) I'm doing my rap. For K.

ZOE: Not now you're not.

(*BRADLEY storms to the CD, switches it off, and goes into the house. K gets up, gets his bag.*)

K: (*To ZOE.*) I'm going. Sorry. Tell Lee.

ZOE: Tell him what?

(*K heads into the entry.*)

ZOE: *Tell him what K!?*

K: He'll understand.

ZOE: No, that's the point, he won't, *I* don't. I still don't know what the fuck you came back for.

(*He stops.*)

K: I wanted to make things right. I wanted to let you see; who I am.

ZOE: *What?* The only good reason you can have for coming back is to give yourself up.

K: That's going backwards.

ZOE: *Forwards,* all the time, me and Lee, I tell him, it's what we do.

K: Zo, you can't even live your own lives and now you're in charge of someone else's! (*He nods at her pregnant belly.*) What sort of a fuck up are you going to make of that? (*Beat. She punches at him.*)

ZOE: *Bastard...*

(*K doesn't react, breathes. She keeps punching.*) You think you know all the answers...

K: Not really.

ZOE: Yeah, *always,* like you know all the fucking answers. 'Beaches, mountains'... And what makes you so perfect, who's going to love you, who's going to have your kids, knowing what you've done?... Me and Lee hate the fucking thought of you. You're scum, you always have been, you're a bully, and you're a user...

K: Not me.

ZOE: Yeah. And now you're a murderer, and you don't even care. (*Beat.*) You killed that lad.

K: No.

ZOE: You killed him, and we're not going to hide it anymore, let everyone see...let Bradley see what you're really like. Martin Merrill, / his name was in the paper.

K: I don't remember...

ZOE: He got mouthy at us, he was pissed, we were all pissed. You'd been out of prison a day, and you couldn't fucking resist it could you?...You hit him, your fist. And he went down.

K: Not me.

ZOE: Like a bag of shit. You stamped on him...

K: Talk later...

ZOE: *Now.* I see it when I'm asleep, your face, like there's nothing can break it...the rage... The lad's on the ground, coughing blood. I saw him gasping and you got his head, smashed it up and down, one, two, three, four, five, six, seven, eight, I counted nine...on the pavement, on the kerb, blood in that Martin lad's ears... Lee tried to drag you off, you hit him too. K is for King. I get it in my fucking head, we used to chant it when we were kids. The girls all said it when we kissed you down the field.

(*Silence.*)

ZOE: You killed that lad because you could. The day they put you in court, don't let anyone try and defend you.
(*Silence. Eventually...*)
Go to the police and tell them what you did.
(*Long long silence. Until...*)

K: (*K turns for his bag.*) Plane.

ZOE: K.
(*ZOE steps towards K. He is staring at his bag, aware of ZOE boring holes into him.*)
You need to go to the pigs Kev.

K: Think all this...like it'll make you...think you're innocent?
(*Beat.*)

ZOE: We *are* fucking innocent.
(*K forces the words out.*)

K: ...won't work...not like that.

ZOE: (*Grabbing at her belly.*) *Well then I don't have this.*
(*She starts hitting herself in the stomach. Instantly, K grabs at her, trying to stop her.*)

K: Lee!!...Lee...fuck's sake...!!
(*LEE and BRADLEY come piling out of the house. LEE grabs at ZOE. She lets her fists fly both sides, punching the shit out of whoever tries to hold her. As LEE takes over trying to calm ZOE, K watches, disturbed, as LEE shields himself and takes the punches, the pain breaking all over him, but he won't move until ZOE's violence becomes exhausted and she stops. Silence. ZOE holds her belly, gasping for air.*)

LEE: What's she doing?

BRADLEY: S'alright.
(*BRADLEY is calm, and holds ZOE's hand.*)
...breathe bro......
(*Silence.*
K has his bag. He takes out his return plane ticket, moves towards LEE.)

K: (*To LEE.*) I want you to come back with me.

ZOE: (*Calmer now, taking in air.*) Fuck you...fuck...
(*Breathes.*) ...go to the police...... Do it for me and Lee...
(*Pause .*)

K: ...done things...since that Martin....done good... Made better, the evil...the fucking...

(*Long silence. K stares at LEE, looks back to ZOE who watches him. LEE goes to K, unsure of K, a feeling that his friend is about to go again. They share a look, and K turns away. He goes. LEE stands at the gate, watching K go. Silence.*)

LEE: What happened?

ZOE: (*To BRADLEY.*) You need to go back to mum and dad.

BRADLEY: Not now bro.

ZOE: Yeah, now. We've got stuff to sort out.

BRADLEY: Like what?... Has K really gone to the police? Bet he doesn't say anything. I wouldn't. I'd tell them to get fucked.

ZOE: Brad...

BRADLEY: I would bro: 'Get fucked, yeah?'

ZOE: Just go.

BRADLEY: In a minute. What's been going on?

LEE: Nothing.

BRADLEY: Stop making out like I'm not here. Is K coming back?

(*Pause.*)

LEE: Just piss off, yeah?

(*BRADLEY goes into the house.*)

(*To ZOE.*) You alright?

ZOE: Dizzy.

LEE: Drink some more water. Heat. I'll ring the docs, get you checked out.

ZOE: I'm alright.

(*BRADLEY comes back out, packing a few last things into her holdall. She adjusts her headphones, grabs her bag.*)

BRADLEY: I'm going.

ZOE: Right.

BRADLEY: Bus fare.

(*ZOE looks to LEE. He digs into his pocket, chucks her a pound coin.*)

LEE: Straight home, and no going near that Black House.

BRADLEY: Like you know what's best for me? (*To ZOE.*) Can't I stay? Please.

ZOE: No. You'll be alright.

(*ZOE stands, goes into the house. BRADLEY watches her go inside.*)

BRADLEY: (*Calling to ZOE.*) Did you see my latest steps? (*No answer.*)

LEE: Just piss off, yeah?

(*BRADLEY does a blast of a breakdance, down, round, gives LEE the finger, and then she's gone.*

But outside in the street, BRADLEY goes nowhere. She sits, lights up a cigarette, and sits with it between her lips, leaning her head back against a lamp post, letting the tears flow.

In the yard, LEE surveys the barbecue.)

Look at this shit.

(*LEE watches the sky, watching as the clouds cover the sun. Outside in the street, BRADLEY stubs out her ciggie and goes, headphones on. ZOE comes back out, clutching a book full of paper cuttings.*)

Rain.

(*She follows LEE's gaze.*)

ZOE: No.

(*She puts the book down.*)

LEE: What's that?

ZOE: I followed everything...after he was killed, all the articles, where he lived, he was good at football, played for the county... Stuff about his mum and dad...

(*LEE looks through the book, pulling out various articles.*)

LEE: You're mental.

(*LEE works at the flower bed, digging with a trowel at the earth.*)

ZOE: His dad worked on FiveFields, did the maintenance in our old flats.

LEE: Yeah? (*Quietly.*) Fuck.

ZOE: I want to go and see his mum and dad.

LEE: Eh!

ZOE: They need to know.

LEE: And say what? We let him die.

ZOE: *No....* I want...like with our kid, when it's growing up, I want to know everything it does, where it's going, what it's doing. They'll want to know won't they? How it happened. I'm going to see them.

LEE: *Fuck's sake.* I want to have a sit down in the new house, you know what I'm saying. Couldn't enjoy it knowing K was coming.

ZOE: But we still can't, can we? Not yet.

(*No answer.*)

So after Martin's parents, I want us to go to the police.

LEE: *What!?...* Jesus, you can't go running round seeing everyone. The Feds'll come, yeah? K'll tell them where we are.

ZOE: Why not?

LEE: Cos I don't walk into any fucking pig station.

ZOE: Since when?

LEE: All my life.

ZOE: *All your life.* Lee, you're 24, this isn't...what you've been doing... Being 24 isn't your life.

LEE: If I go in there I'll be a laughing stock. 'Old Lee, he turned himself in.'

ZOE: We'll do it together, it's not just you; it's you and me.

LEE: You're knackered. Kid's popping in a few weeks.

ZOE: Whatever they say to us, whatever trouble we're in...we need to get it over with.

(*She goes to the gate, waits.*)

(*To LEE.*) Are you coming?

(*No answer from LEE, and so ZOE turns, and leaves the yard.*)

LEE: (*Calling.*) Zo...

(*No answer. She is gone. LEE holds the book of cuttings. He chucks it down. He looks to the gate, ZOE hasn't returned. He prowls the space, goes to the gate where he stops, looking out into the street. He sits on the cool box.*

Long silence.

He looks to the gate, back to the house, the yard, and back again to the gate, sizing it up, choosing, willing himself to go, to join ZOE.)